George Tierney

The Real Situation of the East-India Company

Considered, with respect to their rights and privileges, under the operation of the late acts of Parliament, establishing a board of control and a committee of secrecy

George Tierney

The Real Situation of the East-India Company
Considered, with respect to their rights and privileges, under the operation of the late acts of Parliament, establishing a board of control and a committee of secrecy

ISBN/EAN: 9783337152406

Printed in Europe, USA, Canada, Australia, Japan

Cover: Foto ©Suzi / pixelio.de

More available books at **www.hansebooks.com**

THE
REAL SITUATION
OF THE
EAST-INDIA COMPANY

CONSIDERED, WITH RESPECT TO

THEIR RIGHTS AND PRIVILEGES,

Under the Operation of the late Acts of Parliament,

ESTABLISHING

A BOARD OF CONTROUL

AND

A COMMITTEE OF SECRECY.

TO WHICH IS ADDED

AN APPENDIX,

CONTAINING

ORIGINAL PAPERS,

Relative to the Proceedings of the COURT OF DIRECTORS, and the RIGHT HON. COMMISSIONERS for THE AFFAIRS OF INDIA.

THE SECOND EDITION.

By GEORGE TIERNEY, Esq.

LONDON:
Printed for J. DEBRETT, Piccadilly, 1787.

THE REAL SITUATION

OF THE

EAST INDIA COMPANY.

FEBRUARY 12, 1786.

IN the course of the debate which took place at the India House on Wednesday last, I was once or twice on the point of intruding on the attention of the Court. I heard myself accused of having petulantly joined the opposition; I was arraigned for an apparent desertion of former principles; I was described as having assisted in the call of a General Court, from a wish to encumber the wheels of Government, and perplex the affairs of the Company; in a word, every taunt was thrown out, which could be supposed to irritate me into hasty recrimination, or betray me into an unguarded warmth of reply which might have afforded an advantage to my enemies. It is with real satisfaction that on my return home I recollect myself to have withstood all these provocations, and that I can now, without any fear of partial misrepresentation, or apprehension of being interrupted by prejudice, dispassionately take up my pen to state to the world at large, the true grounds on which my conduct with regard to the Company has been founded.

In the first place, as to the charge of acting from factious motives, and having changed my principles from pique or unsteadiness, I beg leave to say that I throw back the insinuation with contempt. I maintain my sentiments on the subject of the different India Bills to have been invariably the same. I opposed with every faculty I possessed, what I conceived to be an unwarrantable and violent encroachment on the part of Mr. Fox. I stood forward against his Bill, because I thought it an unjustifiable infringement on a Charter which was not proved to be forfeited, and because I thought it might be the means of giving to one branch of the Legislature a weight of influence dangerous to the authority of the other two. I still avow the terms, and am proud of the part I took against that measure; but I should little deserve the approbation which those sentiments at the time procured me, could I have hesitated to resist the same violence, because it was offered in a different shape by different men. Within a few days after the Portland Administration was dismissed, I attended the Committee of Proprietors appointed to watch over the rights of the Company, and heard with surprise the concessions which were about to be made to the new Government; but it was not with *silent* surprize.—I instantly *opposed* such language. Mr. Johnstone was in the Chair, and, if his present state of health would happily admit of such an appeal, I would call upon him to vouch for the truth of what I have here asserted. The memory of my friends will, however, voluntarily do justice to the consistency of my sentiments on the occasion, and the recollection of my enemies will perhaps be quickened, when I remind them that it was on that

that very subject I had the bad fortune to attract the censure of the late Mr. Atkinson, and to smart under the correction of his superior abilities.— Again I must repeat, that my opposition has uniformly been levelled at the measure and not the men.

But I shall be asked, why, it is that my attack on the present Bill has been so long delayed? I will meet the question fairly.

At the period of the great Revolution in Politics 1783-4, Gentlemen were accustomed by some strange fatality never to censure Mr. Fox without praising Mr. Pitt. It seemed to be with them a necessary consequence, that to instance the temerity of the one, was to demonstrate the moderation of the other, and that to prove Mr. Fox unfit to be entrusted with the management of the East India Company, was to establish his rival as the most proper person to overlook all their affairs. Hence, though they certainly never could have expected to see the present Bill, while they remembered Mr. Pitt's language with regard to the one which was rejected, there were many reasons why their feelings could not be openly declared. After the praises they had so wantonly lavished on the new Minister, it was almost impossible for them, though they saw the danger, to retreat—perhaps too it may be said that their retreat was cut off, there being no *third* party to receive them. They might be stunned by the blow which was so unexpectedly given, and by so sudden and unlooked-for an assault rendered incapable of resistance, or, even when they recovered themselves, false shame might operate, and those who had been so very eager to shew how warily they had detected the designs of their avowed enemy,

enemy, might be unwilling to acknowledge how much they found themselves deceived in the profeſſions of their ſuppoſed friends. Be this as it may, certain it is that all the circumſpection, vigilance, and nice ſenſe of right, which had ſo laudably diſtinguiſhed both the Directors and Proprietors, on a ſudden dwindled into nothing. It was boldly aſſerted that what was done, was done with the conſent of the Company,—no contradiction was given, and the Bill paſſed.

At ſuch a ſeaſon, and with the minds of men ſo diſpoſed, would it not have been the height of abſurdity to have come forward in oppoſition to the meaſure? Should I not have been told, that narrow notions of excluſive privilege were to be laid aſide; that both parties had ſeen the neceſſity of abandoning the ſtrict queſtion of right; that the occaſion for a Parliamentary Controul of ſome kind was admitted on all hands; that the purity of Mr. Pitt's character gave ſuch a ſanction to any Board of which he was a member, that ſuſpicion was not allowable; that candour required the Bill ſhould at leaſt have a trial; and that it would be unfair to preſume without proofs, that jealouſies would ariſe between the Court of Directors and the new Commiſſioners, or that the latter had any idea of deviating from what the India Company conceived to be the ſpirit of the act, and were themſelves willing to receive as ſuch. ———Will any impartial man ſay, that the oppoſition of a few Proprietors would not, when theſe arguments prevailed, have been an idle and unprofitable attempt? It would indeed at that time have been a ridiculous one—But the caſe at this day is different. We are now able to decide upon cauſe and effect together. The unguarded confidence

which

which was reposed on the sanction of Mr. Pitt's name, cannot obliterate certain papers signed "*Henry Dundas.*" It is no longer a question what a daring Board of Controul *might do*,—we see what even the present unassuming Commissioners *have done*. What formerly would have been termed arguments of malicious theory, are now inferences of recorded practice; and as, by dear bought experience, we are at length freed from the blind devotion which was paid to the measure at its outset, I trust we are capable of examining dispassionately the consequences which have accompanied its progress.

One word more and I proceed to the business. In what I have hereafter to say I must be allowed to lay in my claim to credit with the candid part of the world. Throughout the whole of my conduct relative to this subject I will be bold to assert, that I have acted, however impoliticly, as an honest and independent man, and that the Proprietors of India Stock were the last set of persons in the world from whom I had reason to have expected unkind insinuations. It is rather an ungrateful return to one who has been a volunteer in their cause, and who is not conscious how the part he has acted can be attributed to any unworthy motives. But this is a point I need not argue. Let my views be conjectured from the means I take to gratify them. I opposed Mr. Fox in the plenitude of his power; I attack the present Commissioners with the sceptre in their hand. Whether or no, in so doing, I either have served or may serve the India Company, I will not venture to pronounce, but I am sure, if my object is of a selfish nature, my method of obtaining my wishes has nothing but its novelty to recommend it.

I now

I now proceed to examine into the real situation of the India Company, under the operation and effect of the acts of the 24th and 26th of Geo. III. as far as they relate to the Board of Controul and the Court of Directors.

The principles of the first of these bills as stated in the House of Commons were these— to vest in a Board of Commissioners a right to superintend and controul the proceedings of the Court of Directors on *all political questions*; but to leave *the enjoyment of the patronage*, and *the management of the commerce, exclusively in the former possessors*. These I maintain to have been the out-lines on which the bill was professed to be drawn; so that the four-and-twenty Directors were still to hold their ostensible authority, actual influence and commercial privileges, with this limitation, that their dispatches relative to the **civil or military** government or revenues of the territorial possessions were to be submitted to the Board of Controul, whose constitution and powers are thus defined.

" His Majesty is to appoint six Privy Counsel-
" lors, of whom one of the Secretaries of State,
" and the Chancellor of the Exchequer for the
" time being shall be two, to be Commissioners
" for the Affairs of India.

" Any three of them shall form a Board, and
" in the absence of the Secretary of State, and
" the Chancellor of the Exchequer, the senior
" of the Commissioners, according to his rank
" in appointment, shall be President.

" In case the said Board shall at any time
" be equally divided, the then President shall
" have the casting voice.

" It

"His Majesty may revoke the commission at pleasure, and appoint new commissioners.

"The Board are empowered to superintend, direct and controul all acts, operations, and concerns which in anywise relate to the civil or military government or revenues of the British territorial possessions in India. The Directors are to deliver to the Board copies of all dispatches which they receive from India immediately on their arrival; also copies of all letters, orders, and instructions whatsoever, relating to the civil or military government or revenues of the territorial possessions, proposed to be dispatched to India, and the said Directors shall obey all orders from the Board relative thereto.

"The Court of Directors shall, without delay, forward their dispatches as they are approved or amended by the Board of Controul, unless, on any representation of the said Directors, the Commissioners may think proper to order an alteration to be made.

"The Court of Directors, on receiving orders from the Board which relate to points, *in their opinion, not connected with the civil or military government or revenues, may apply by petition to the King in Council, who shall decide whether the same be, or be not connected with the civil or military government or revenues, which decision shall be conclusive.*

"The Directors are to choose, from amongst themselves, a Secret Committee, of not more than three.

"*If the Board of Controul shall be of opinion that the subject matter of their deliberations, concerning the making war or peace, or negotiating with any of the native Princes or States in India,*

" shall require secrecy, they may send secret orders
" to the Secret Committee, who, without disclosing
" them, shall transmit their orders in the usual
" form, according to the instructions of the Board
" to the respective governments and presidencies,
" and the said governments and presidencies shall
" pay obedience to such dispatches, and shall return
" their answers, sealed, to the said Secret Com-
" mittee.

" The several governments and presidencies are
" required to pay the same obedience to all orders
" signed by the said Secret Committee, as if such
" orders had been issued by the Court of Directors.

" Nothing in the Act shall extend to give to
" the Board of Controul the power of nomi-
" nating or appointing any of the servants of
" the said United Company.

Such are the powers of the Board of Controul, and so are they defined in the Act of Parliament.

The first observation which must occur to every man who reads the different clauses, is the very shallow security given for the Board not interfering with the commerce. For my own part, indeed, I do not exactly comprehend how, in the nature of things, it ever can be practicable, totally to *separate* the *commercial* from the *civil* and *revenue department*. That the trade of the Company may be ably carried on by twenty-four gentlemen, acting in concert with, and under the direction of a superior Board, I can readily conceive; but to suppose it can continue to thrive under the management of a set of men who have no authority, acting in opposition to a Board who have the entire superintendance of all our territories in India, who have the right of making war and peace, the arrangement of all

matters

matters of revenue, and the office of negotiating with every power in the country from whence this trade is to flow, is a position which I should beg leave to question. It is to be considered, that our connection with India stands upon a very different footing from what it originally did. Commerce and territory are now so intimately blended, that their respective consequence must, perhaps, entirely depend on their *united* exertions. " The conquest of Bengal," says the Abbé Raynal, " without making any essential
" alteration in the external form of the English
" Company, has produced a material change in
" the object of it. They are no longer a *com-*
" *mercial society*, they are *a territorial power*
" who make the most of their revenues by the
" assistance of a traffic that formerly was their
" sole existence, and which, notwithstanding the
" extension it has received, is no more than an
" accessary in the various combinations of their
" present real grandeur." And again, the same author, speaking of the Supreme Council established by the Act of 1773, after stating to what its authority extends, adds, " though the ope-
" rations of commerce be not immediately
" under the inspection of this Council, yet it
" has in reality the decision of them; because
" having the sole disposal of the public revenues,
" it can grant or refuse advances at pleasure." I mention thus much rather as a matter of amusing speculation than as a point which it is at present necessary to argue, for I contend that the question is, not whether it be *possible* to separate the commerce from the civil government and revenue, but whether such a distinction *is favoured* by the present Act of Parliament.

C   Whenever

Whenever the intentions of men are fair and open they will express themselves in terms plain, and unequivocal. If I mean that certain things should be performed according to my professions, my orders for the performance will naturally run almost in the language of my promise. An evasive execution is worse than a denial of the contract, because it avoids the test of direct enquiry, treacherously withholds what it dares not openly refuse, harasses one party and disgraces the other.

When this bill was introduced, in order to attract the praises that are bestowed on moderation, and to gain the confidence of the people by an affected display of disinterested motives, it was said, " we do not mean to go the violent length " of our predecessors; God forbid that we " should touch the *trade* of the Company; *that* " we intend should still remain exclusively their " own." Let it be so enacted then—No! when we come to reduce these professions to writing, they run thus: " In case we should ever think " proper, in our dispatches, to give directions " which relate to trade as well as government, " it shall not be lawful for you to say at once, " that we have exceeded our powers, and inter- " fered with your commerce, but you shall ap- " peal to the King in Council, to *know whether* " *we have or not!*" Here is the whole security the Company have, and even this clause I think I shall, in the sequel, be able to prove is virtually done away. An appeal! from six Privy Counsellors, two of whom are in the Cabinet, to the King in Council!—The decision that would be given is about as difficult to be guessed at, as the result of a Dean and Chapter's deliberations

when

when they affemble to elect a Bifhop. An appeal! to beg his Majefty will *explain to four-and-twenty merchants* what things are to be underftood as *relating to trade!*—It is as ridiculous as if the *Privy Council* were to apply to the *India Houfe* for a definition of *prerogative*. To argue this claufe ferioufly would be to give it a degree of confequence to which it is not entitled. It needs but to be read to be proved an infult to our underftanding, and to make us feel that the real regard of Mr. Pitt for the rights of the Company, when reduced to practice, can only be equalled by that *difinterefted* zeal with which Mr. Dundas has the goodnefs to accept the very troublefome office of fuperintending the affairs of India, *without falary* or *profpect of reward!*

Having recapitulated the powers of the Board of Controul, as defined by the act of parliament, and fhewn the happy method by which that act gives fecurity to *one* of the leading principles on which it avowedly was recommended to the Legiflature for adoption, I next proceed to point out in what manner the authority of the Commiffioners has been exerted on the *other* principle of the bill,—that of fuperintending the *political* concerns of the Company; and on this head I affert, that the very firft exercife of their office was *a direct contradiction and defiance of the words of the act*, as well as a palpable *neglect of the intereft of the Company*. To prove my firft affertion I cite the claufe in queftion, to prove my fecond I refer to the declaration of the Court of Directors, and I then appeal, for a fair decifion, to the common fenfe of every man who perufes what I am about to write.

There were certain enormous sums of money claimed by some British subjects at Madrass, as being due from the Nabob of Arcot. These debts are classed in three divisions; one called the Loan of 1767, the other the Cavalry Loan, and the third the Consolidated Debt of 1777, amounting in the whole to 70 lacks of pagodas, or 2,800,000l, Of this sum the debt of 1777 constituted the greater part; that is to say, in 1781, it stood at 50 lacks of pagodas, or 2,000,000l, bearing an interest at 12 *per cent*. The reflections that had at different times been cast on the nature and secret history of these transactions did not redound much to the credit of the claims; most of them were much involved in an ambiguous obscurity, but *the loan of 1777* was wrapped in *total darkness*. The Directors say, " Although we have repeatedly " written to the Nabob, and to our servants, " respecting the debt, yet we have *never been* " *able to trace the origin thereof, or to obtain* " *any satisfactory information upon the subject*."

When it is understood that the *public debt* from the Nabob to the Company (for the arrears of his current payments, and the expences incurred in defending the Carnatic) is computed by the Directors as being nothing short of three millions sterling; and when it is stated, that, taken in the most favourable point of view, the net revenues of the Nabob do not exceed 30 lacks, or 1,200,000l, the reader will easily perceive the embarrassment that must proceed from outstanding *private* claims being pressed upon him to so great an amount as above related, and how necessary it was, in order to an equitable arrangement, finally to ascertain their validity

validity and extent. Where the greater part of the fortunes of so many British subjects was concerned, it certainly would have been unfair, on the bare suspicion of collusion and fraud, to disallow the whole claims of the private creditors; but, on the other hand, justice to the Company equally required, that the Directors should not suffer the payment of their public debt, bearing *no* interest, to be protracted, by admitting to a participation of the * fund to be established by the Nabob for the discharge of his incumbrances, claims to an enormous amount carrying *an interest of* 12 *per cent.* of which neither the origin nor legality could be traced. The Nabob's own admission of their validity weighed but little, for the very ground of objection to them was, that they were a *collusive shuffle between the debtor and the creditor*: So that it became an information necessarily to be required, *what sums had been actually* and *bona fide advanced*, in order that they might be distinguished from others which shrunk from inspection, and had continually avoided every test of open examination †.

* The Nabob is to assign twelve lacks annually, from his revenues, towards the liquidation of his debt.

† In stating this abstract of the history of the debts, my only view has been to comprize, in a small compass, sufficient to enable the reader to comprehend the object of the clause in the act. Those who have taken the trouble to examine into these transactions, know, that to enter upon the merits at large would, in itself, occupy a volume. I have endeavoured faithfully to give the brief outlines of the business, and shall only further observe, that in mentioning the imputations which have been cast on the nature and origin of the debts, I have contented myself with adopting much milder language than either the Directors, the Presidency of Fort St. George, or even Mr. Dundas. *Vide* the 4th Report of the Secret Committee, and the Appendix to it.

Such

Such being the state of the question, let us proceed to examine the conduct of the Legislature thereon.

By the 37th clause of the act, (see the Appendix, No. I. 1.) the Court of Directors are instructed to take the origin and justice of these demands into their consideration, as far as the materials they are in possession of will enable them to do, and to direct their Presidency abroad to *complete the investigation*, and then, in concert with the Nabob, to establish a fund for the discharge of those debts *which shall be justly due*, in such a manner as may be consistent with the rights of the Company, the security of the creditors, and the honor and dignity of the Nabob.

I ask any unprejudiced man whether, having read the facts which gave rise to the introduction of the clause, and the terms that are adopted in it, he would not naturally conceive the meaning of the Legislature to have been this: " We refer
" the arrangement of these disputed claims *ex-*
" *pressly* to the *Court of Directors*, and we mark
" out the *precise manner* in which they are to dis-
" charge this commission. Their first great object
" must be thoroughly to *investigate* the *origin* and
" *justice* of the debts, and having *ascertained* such
" of them as shall be *justly due*, proceed to settle
" with the Nabob some mode for putting them in
" a regular train of payment. But in adjusting
" this train of payment, the Directors must take
" care, first, that it does not interfere with the rights
" and claims of the Company; next, that the
" creditors be secured according to the fair priority
" of their demands; and lastly, not suffer their
" attention to either the rights of the Company,
" or the claims of the British subjects, to militate
" against

" againſt the proper honour and dignity which the
" Nabob ought always to preſerve."

Acting apparently under theſe ideas, the Court of Directors prepared a diſpatch which, previous to its being ſent to India, was ſubmitted to the Board of Controul. It ſtates (ſee Appendix No. I. 2.) that they had taken the demands into conſideration as far as they had materials, which materials they quote and comment upon. They then ſay, That " being in a ſtate of uncertainty as
" to the origin of the demands both of the old and
" new creditors, (*particularly the latter, which pre-*
" *cludes them from judging of the juſtice thereof.*)" they direct their Preſident and Council at Fort St. George, to enter into " a full *examination* of
" the *origin* and *juſtice* of them; whether the ſums
" were *really and bona fide advanced*, and alſo the
" name of each individual creditor who ſhall
" prove his debt to the ſatisfaction of the ſaid
" Preſident and Council." This done, the next orders are, to tranſmit the whole of the proceedings to the Governor General and Council, who, having taken the ſame into their conſideration, are directed to make the final diſtribution and award according to the proviſions of the Act of Parliament.

Theſe orders the Board of Controul *totally expunge*, and ſubſtitute others in their place in *direct contradiction* both to the *words* and *the ſpirit* of the clauſe referred to. It was the will of the Legiſlature, that the debts ſhould be firſt proved and then ſecured—It was the pleaſure of the great Commiſſioner that they ſhould be firſt ſecured, and then ſtand admitted till they were diſproved.—Fortunately for Mr. Benfield and his friends, the fiat of the latter carried moſt authority.

The

The Paragraphs as altered by the Board of Controul run thus: (fee the Appendix, No. I. 3.) The Loan of 1767, and the Cavalry Loan are at once pronounced *clear* and *indisputable*. They then come to the debt of 1777, amounting to 2,000,000l. and after shewing, that " it was not " in any respect whatever conducted under the " auspices or protection of the Presidency at " Madras;" that it has " no sanction nor autho-" rity," even in the estimation of Mr. Dundas himself; that the means taken to procure the discharge of this unauthorized demand were such as disabled the Nabob from performing his duty to the Company, and that, under all these circumstances, they should " be warranted to refuse " their aid or protection in the recovery of this " loan;"—after thus criminating the whole transaction, they proceed to give it their—*support and assistance*. When they consider " *how inexpedient it is to keep the subject longer afloat*;" how much the final conclusion of the business will tend to promote " *circulation of property*;" when they consider too, " that the *debtor concurs with the creditor* in establishing the justice of these debts, and how little ground there is to expect any substantial good to result from an unlimited *investigation*,"—they resolved *to recognize the justice of them*, and to extend to them *that protection*, which upon more forcible grounds they saw cause to allow to the other two classes. The Presidency are, however, directed to receive any complaints against the debts of 1777, either from the Nabob, other creditors injured by their being so admitted, or by other persons having a proper interest, or stating a reasonable ground of objection. The Board then declare the sentence of arrangement as to priority in point of payment, and having done this, the Right Honourable Commissioners triumphantly pronounce their decree to be " founded in justice," and magisterially command, that whoever shall dare to disturb it shall " be dismissed the " service, and sent home to England."

In the Appendix (No. I. 4.) the reader will find the representation of the Court of Directors against this extraordinary exercise of power, in which they most truly observe, that those demands, the *justice* of which the act required them to *investigate*, were, by the amended paragraphs, at once *substantiated without examination*. But they add, " to these your appropriations of the " fund, *our duty requires that we should state our* " *strongest dissent*. Our right to be paid the ar- " rears of those expences, (by which almost the " country and all the property connected with it " were preserved from falling a prey to a foreign " conqueror) surely stands paramount to all " claims for former debts upon the revenues of " a country so preserved, even if the Legislature " had not *expressly limited the assistance to be* " *given to the private creditors to be such as* " *should be consistent with our own rights*. They then go at large into a detail of calculations (which see in the Appendix) and conclude with the following forcible inference: " thus " the public debt, carrying no interest, will be " protracted to afford a preference to private " debts, consisting of different descriptions, on a " part of which claims *the Board have declared*, " *they were contracted contrary to the public* " *orders of the Company, and therefore to have* " *[illegible]*
" [illegible]"

D

The Appendix (No I. 5.) contains the rejoinder of the Board of Controul to this representation, in which, after only giving way in one point, (viz. that the debt shall be made up to the year 1784 with simple instead of compound interest,) they attempt to deal out some comfort by assuring the Directors that they have the *strongest grounds to believe that the private debts will be considerably less than they are now computed, and consequently the Company's proportion of the twelve lacks will be larger than in the estimate is supposed. They then tell them, that being of opinion there is not any room for objecting to the arrangement, they have made " no alteration in the general out-lines of " it," and desire that it may be forthwith transmitted to India,—and so ends the disposal of upwards of £.200,000 of secret claims, by the penetration of the Honourable Commissioners discovering, that " no substantial good could re- " sult from an *investigation* into those debts," of which, by the *Act of Parliament*, the Court of Directors are expressly enjoined to *enquire the origin and justice.*

* *Where* did the Right Hon. Commissioner obtain these *strong grounds of belief?* Are there some papers at the India-House which the Court of Directors have never seen? Is Lord Macartney's statement to be considered as fallacious. Or, does he derive his information from some more conv..ch..., authority than any *public* document, which authority he does not think proper to bring forth? If, in his volunteer researches for the good of the Company, he has discovered any fortunate clue by which new light is thrown on their dark transactions, surely common justice required that he should have let the Directors into the secret.

I said I would prove the conduct of the Board of Controul to be in this instance contrary to the letter and spirit of the law, as well as injurious to the Company, and I trust I shall be allowed to have fulfilled my promise, at least until a *hasty admission* of a debt can be construed as a *complete investigation* of it, and until the substantial calculations of the Court of Directors shall be opposed by something more convincing than *strong grounds of belief.*—I must now take the liberty to offer a few observations on the subject, which, in order to draw the reader's attention as little as possible from the consideration of the facts, I have hitherto refrained from.

In the first place then, two classes out of these debts " appear clear and indisputable," but the *third* has neither " sanction nor authority" from the Board of Controul, the Court of Directors, or the Presidency of Madrafs, for which reasons, (this being " an arrangement founded in jus-" tice,") *the same protection is to be extended to it which has been allowed to the other two!* The vulgar way of coming at the reality of a contested debt is to make the creditor *prove* it, but the new method adopted here scorns this old fashioned practice, and *admits the justice of the demand* till somebody shall think proper to state a reasonable ground of objection. Either way this part of the arrangement is culpable: if the creditor is once able fairly to substantiate his claim, it is cruel to subject him to after objections; if his debt cannot be satisfactorily proved, it is unjust to adopt a general presumption in his favour. —But I believe the objections to this arrangement will in India be but few; shallow indeed must the policy of the creditors be, if they do not secure the happy turn in their favor, and fortify, beyond the reach of future attacks, the ground the Right Honourable Commissioners have given them. A few straggling malecontents, too insignificant to be enlisted in the grand combination, may perhaps mutter a threat or two, but there it will end. Without giving them the trouble to tell all they know, their grievances may be redressed, and at the same time two of the great objects which the Board of Controul profess to have in view in this decision will be obtained —" Tran-" quillity" will be preserved by " the circula-" tion of property."

Let me now sum up the result of the business, and I will quit this part of my subject. I have proved the interference of the Board of Controul to have been exerted in a manner *contrary* to the *positive instructions of the Act of Parliament*, and *injurious to the interests of the Company*. The Commissioners have not exercised a power of revising and amending the dispatches of the Directors, but they have totally expunged their whole orders, and substituted others in their room founded on principles diametrically different. They have not confined themselves to the superintending a political negotiation to which the Directors might be held incompetent, but they have opposed and counteracted them in the discharge of an office delegated to them by the Legislature, familiar to their capacities from their habits of life, strictly within their department as a pecuniary transaction, and proposed to be executed in a manner to which no objection could be made, because it was marked out and sanctioned by the hand of Parliament itself.

itself.—After such an encroachment, what may not be dreaded? If the Board so daringly exert their authority in contradiction to the express provisions of the act, what will they not attempt on points whereon the Legislature has been silent? If, where the powers of the Court of Directors are ascertained, the Commissioners can annihilate them with impunity, what shall become of those privileges which are only obliquely recognized in ambiguous terms?—In vain may the Right Honourable arbitrators attempt to shelter this measure under the pleas of "expediency," and the necessity of coming to "a final conclusion;"—I say the instance before us establishes a precedent by which the whole property of the East India Company falls under the controul of these new sovereigns; I assert that the conduct of the Board breathes defiance to the *words* of the Act of Parliament; and as to the *spirit* of it, let me only ask if it can be supposed that the House of Commons, when they ordered the Directors to investigate the origin and justice of suspicious claims to the amount of millions, could have designed that Mr. Dundas and his colleagues should extend a sudden protection to them without examination or enquiry?

The powers of the Court of Directors having been thus in pecuniary matters demolished, the next point to which I request the attention of the Reader relates to another privilege of the Company—that of enforcing discipline in India, and preserving obedience and subordination amongst the servants abroad.

By the 17th section of the act it was declared, that the Board of Controul shall not have the appointment of any offices, and when, added to this, there was a right vested in the Directors to dismiss from their service whomsoever they chose, it was imagined that the Bill acted up to the professions of its framers, and that the Company were effectually secured in the possession of their former patronage. Ingenuity contrived however to discover a method by which, without claiming any power to nominate, the Board of Controul assumed to themselves the means of rendering the appointments an honour or a disgrace, and teaching the servants in India, that though the Directors gave them their offices, they were to be accountable for their conduct in the discharge of them to a *superior authority*. The right of * *dismissing* the Board already shared with the Directors, but from the right of *appointment* they had the mortification to feel themselves clearly excluded. The discerning Commissioner saw that if this power was suffered to remain pure and unfettered with the Company, they would possess a degree of respectability, and maintain an independent rank in the eyes of their servants, highly prejudicial to the Majesty of the Board of Controul. By some means or other therefore such a privilege was to be contracted and enfeebled, and if this remaining jewel in the Court of Directors could not be purloined, it was at any rate necessary that its value should be depreciated and its lustre offuscd. An opportunity was not long wanting to carry this plan into execution.

* Appendix, No. 1. 3. "And even that "any creditor shall be bound to accept, or at all "disturb the arrangement we have [illegible]

A Colonel Rofs, by a refolution of the Court of Directors, was permitted "to return to India as Lieutenant Colonel and Chief Engineer at Madras, but *not allowed to rank in the infantry corps on that eftablifhment.*" This exception thwarting his object, which was to obtain the advanced rank of *Colonel in the army by brevet*, he petitioned the Directors, who refufed to comply with his requeft, and twice put a negative upon the application. Upon his arrival at Madras, however, the Colonel renewed his folicitations to the Prefident and Council, and endeavoured to obtain from *them* what he had been fo pofitively refufed *here*. The Prefidency, in their letter to the Company, make mention of this new application, to which the Directors, after ftating the circumftances as above, conclude their anfwer in thefe words: " his (Colonel Rofs's) urging *you* to a " compliance with a requeft which *we* had pre- " vioufly decided on, was highly difrefpectful " to us, and we direct that you acquaint Lieu- " tenant Colonel Rofs of our difapprobation of " his conduct on this occafion." (See Appendix. No. II. 1.)

The Board of Controul having thought proper to *expunge* the whole of this paragraph, becaufe " they cannot concur in the difapprobation of " Colonel Rofs." (See Appendix, No. II. 2.) the Court of Directors, as on the former occafion, prefented a remonftrance on fuch conduct (Appendix, No. II, 3.)—but it unluckily happened that, in their zeal to defend their privileges, they almoft fought the battle of their enemies, by affording them the very opportunity they wifhed, to proclaim officially to the fervants in India that

the

the authority of the Company was *transferred to another quarter.*

The remonstrance of the Directors states, that the mode adopted by Colonel Ross, of " appeal-
" ing from the superior to the inferior authority
" is so destructive of all government, that they
" should think they *abdicated their trust* if such a
" conduct was permitted to pass without cen-
" sure;" and " that a deliberate contempt of their
" authority not only *not disapproved*, but *in-
" directly applauded*, by the Right Hon. Board
" *refusing permission even to reprehend*, must
" lead their servants to imagine, that it is *no
" longer their duty to obey those who possess the
" present authority in Great Britain*, but that
" *they may safely speculate on the probable judgment
" which may be hereafter formed on the propriety
" of the original orders.*"

Had the evil Genius of the India Company himself guided the pen, he could not have written a language more severely to be turned against them than the passages I have above quoted; and to do justice to the Honourable Commissioners, they have not overlooked the advantage that was to be gained.—Whether Colonel Ross was reprehended or not, signified but little; the grand point was, to [illegible] *they [illegible] at what the Board
will [illegible] at all*, and this has been most effec-
tually done. The rejoinder cuts a sting in every word. (See Append., No. II. p.) for
" [illegible]
" [illegible]
" [illegible]
" [illegible]
" [illegible]
" [illegible]

[25]

" *any servant, civil or military*, EXCLUSIVE OF
" THE CONTROUL OF THIS BOARD!—
The obvious inference to be drawn from this in
India must be, that, as the Right Hon. Board
have declared their right of " refusing permission
" even to reprehend," the opinion of the Directors
themselves justifies the servants in being " lead to
" imagine, that it is no longer their duty to obey
" those who possess the present authority in Great
" Britain, but that they may safely speculate on
" the probable judgment which may be hereafter
" formed on the propriety of the original orders."

Here then at once, degraded Company, is a
blow struck at your patronage which leaves it in
a situation but little to be envied. Appoint your
own favourite, and the frowns of the Commissioners may cloud all his fair prospects, and by
one pointed censure for ever crush his hopes of
preferment;—appoint the favourite of the Board,
and he may insult your authority, and subvert
your discipline without your being permitted even
to reprehend him. The odium and the external
forms of patronage you have, but the sweets and
the essential authority of it belong to another.
The flattering approbation that gratifies fidelity,
and the dreaded reprimand that gives vigour to
discipline, are no longer yours: they flow from
another quarter, in opposition to whose decrees,
not even the King can impart encouragement or
rebuke to the military in India. In that branch of
the empire all that either your power, or his Prerogative can in future be entitled to, is the
angry jealousy of unsuccessful candidates, which
will ever attend on the right to appoint, and the
rooted resentments which will necessarily follow the
exercise of the only other privilege you have.—un-
conditionally

conditionally to difmifs. To diftribute the laurel of military achievement, to confer approbation on judicial integrity, and reward the faithful diligence of civil exertion, are ingratiating offices which appertain to Mr. Dundas. True it is, the foldier, the judge, and the governor owe their appointments to you, but they feel that their characters and eftimation with the world depend on higher opinions, and doubtlefs they will pay their court accordingly.

We have now traced the Board of Controul refolutely obtaining the difpofal of millions, and holding themfelves up as the fountain of public condemnation or favour to all the Britifh Settlements in India; what will be faid, when I go on to demonftrate that even thefe ftrides were not long enough for the ambition of fome men, but that, fetting all oppofition at defiance, they perfift in their career, and, more fecurely to carry it on, enable themfelves to act under the fafeguard of a *fworn fecrecy*.

In the recital of the powers of the Board of Controul as defined by the firft Act of Parliament on the fubject, the Reader will find that the Directors were ordered to chufe three from amongft themfelves who were to conftitute a Secret Committee, and, having reminded him of this, I muft beg leave to ftate the claufe which directs the purpofes to which the faid Committee are to be applied, *verbatim*, in order that I may not ftand fufpected of any mifreprefentation. By the 15th fection, it is enacted that, " If the Board *fhall be of* " *opinion*, that the fubject matter of any of their de- " liberations, concerning the levying of war or " making of peace, or *treating or negotiating with* " *any of the native Princes, States, or Powers*, fhall be

" *quire secrecy*, it shall and may be lawful for the
" said Board *to send secret orders and instructions to*
" *the said Secret Committee* for the time being,
" who shall thereupon, *without disclosing the same*,
" transmit their orders and dispatches in the usual
" form, according to the tenor of the said orders
" and instructions of the said Board, to the re-
" spective Government and Presidencies in India ;
" and that the said Governments and Presidencies
" shall *pay a faithful obedience to such orders*
" and *dispatches*, and shall *return their answers*
" sealed, (under cover) with their respective seals
" *to the said Secret Committee* who shall forth-
" with communicate such answers to the said
" Board." I refrained from taking notice of this clause before, because I wished without interruption to bring the narrative down to the period when the *oath of secrecy* was added to it, in order that I might consider it in its state of perfection.

Whether it was owing to any distrust the Board might have in the Gentlemen appointed to compose the Secret Committee, as not thinking them all tried men, or that the great Commissioner found when the Court of Directors got any item of what was going forward they were apt to comment too freely upon it, or that he was angry with the Committee for some hints they had let out, or that he had some master stroke in contemplation which for the good of the Company it was proper they should know nothing of, or which might not be quite calculated for public inspection,— how this might be I cannot presume to say, but early in the last session a clause was introduced into the new act of parliament which compelled every member of the Secret Committee to take a solemn oath, " not to disclose or make

" known

[28]

"known any of the secret orders or instructions
"which might be communicated to him by the
"Commissioners for the Affairs of India, concern-
"ing the levying of war, or making of peace,
"or *treating or negociating* with any of the
"native Princes or States of India, unless he be
"authorized by the said Commissioners to disclose
"and make known the same."

Thus did the Right Hon. Gentleman prudently prepare the way for any new schemes he might have in agitation, and prevent all impertinent observation on his conduct by swearing his agents to secrecy.

————Never, so help you mercy!
How strange or odd so e'er I bear myself,
As I perchance hereafter shall think meet
To put an antick disposition on,————
That you at such times seeing me, never shall,
(With arms encumbered thus or this head shake,
Or by pronouncing of some doubtful phrase,
As, *well, well, we know*—or *we could, if we would*;
Or, *if we list to speak*;—or *there be, an if we might*,
Or such ambiguous givings out) denote
That you know aught of me :—This do ye swear
So grace and mercy at your most need help you.

Here was the final blow given to every privilege of the company, and step by step we have at last seen the real situation to which, by Mr. Pitt's bill, it was meant to reduce the Court of Directors. After the language which had been used with respect to Mr. Fox's rejected measure, it was impossible decently to take the Charter at once, but gradually and underhand it has most effectually been done; and really the proofs

is

is ingenious. First, the King is to appoint six Commissioners, who are to superintend and controul the dispatches of the twenty-four Directors; then these twenty-four Directors are to chuse three of their number who are to form a Secret Committee. This Committee are kept back as a corps of reserve, for some unforeseen emergency—no immediate use appears to have been made of them for a considerable time after their appointment, because to have shewn too early the purposes to which they were to be applied, might have given the alarm before the Right Honourable Gentleman was firm in his seat. The first battles were therefore to be fought with the whole Direction together, and having vanquished them in one engagement, and contrived, though quitting the field, to carry off their colours in the other, the great Commissioner grows weary of these troublesome encounters, feels himself secure in his power, and resolving to manage India more at his ease, at length brings his Secret Committee to the charge, and gives notice, that in future he means to act through them.—Within a few days after the Committee were sworn, the curtain was dropped, and the Directors effectually shut out from all inspection into their affairs.

A dispatch was prepared to be sent to Madras relative to certain arrangements with the Nabob of Arcot of a pecuniary nature, which, according to the orders of the Court of Directors, dated the 9th December, 1784, the Presidency of Fort St. George had previously made some progress in, and were preparing to establish upon a permanent footing. On this dispatch being submitted to the

the Board of Controul for their approbation, they expunge almoſt the whole of it, and then deliver this laconic meſſage: "*As we think it more proper that ſuch inſtructions, as it is now neceſſary to tranſmit upon the ſubject, ſhould go through the channel of your Secret Committee, we ſhall ſend a draft to them for that purpoſe.*"—And, that there may be no miſunderſtanding as to who is Lord paramount of the Board of Controul, Mr. Dundas ſigns firſt, and then *follows* "William Pitt;"—*ego et Rex meus*—firſt "Henry Dundas," *next*, his Majeſty's Prime Miniſter!*

On the receipt of this letter, the Court of Directors took the alarm, and conceiving a *mere pecuniary tranſaction, relative neither to peace nor war*, could not be an object which the legiſlature ever wiſhed to keep the light from, ſimply becauſe it was a tranſaction with a native Prince of India, in addition to the opinion of their own counſel, obtained thoſe of the Attorney and Solicitor General—which ſee in the Appendix No.

---

* As I really thought this muſt have been a miſtake in copying the letter, I took the trouble to enquire into the fact, and will now aſſert, that in the *original* the ſignatures ſtand as I have deſcribed. It is almoſt impoſſible that Mr. Pitt could have aſſiſted at the Board when this famous meſſage was drawn up, notwithſtanding he has ſigned it; becauſe, had he been preſent, he muſt, by the Act of Parliament, have been Preſident, and as ſuch, neceſſarily ſigned *firſt*. I have heard it ſaid, that the way in which buſineſs is tranſacted at the Board of Controul is this—Mr. D. dictates and ſigns the diſpatches, which, having once obtained the ſanction of his _____ are carried round to the other Commiſſioners, who add their ſignatures as a *matter of courſe*. The world will determine whether or not what I have above ſtated gives a colour to this report.

VI.

IV. The three opinions however uniformly agree, that, by the letter of the Act, the Board were authorised to proceed in the manner they did. Mr. Smith, one of the Directors, threw up his office and resigned a station in which he found himself deprived of all information on those subjects which his duty seemed to require him to inspect. (Appendix, No. V. 1.) The General Court came to a strong resolution, that the powers exercised by the Board were subversive of their " chartered rights, and tended to " establish a secret system of government, highly " dangerous to the interests of the public and " Company." (Appendix, V. No. 3.) The Court of Directors deputed the two Chairmen to wait upon Mr. Pitt, to lay the above resolution before him, and ask his assistance in Parliament to explain the powers of the Board of Controul with regard to secret correspondence. To this request, Mr. Pitt, having taken a week to consider of, and most probably to consult with his friend on the subject, returned for answer, that " he did not see any grounds for an application " to Parliament." (Appendix, V. No. 4, 5, 6.) From that day to this, the Board of Controul have been arbitrary monarchs.

I have, in the Appendix, inserted the whole of the proposed dispatch, and marked out the particular passages expunged by the Commissioners, for the satisfaction of the curious reader, and that I may not be accused of keeping any thing back; but I do not here mean to take up time by entering into the detail of the business. My arguments rest not upon the propriety of expunging this or that particular paragraph: it is

the

the *principle* on which the Board acts that I oppose, because a *precedent* is now *established*, by which it will in future only be requisite to connect the subject matter with the name of any native Prince, or State in India, and the key is to be turned on the Court of Directors. Let the most sanguine admirers of Administration peruse the manly opinion of Mr. Rouse, and the excellent and spirited letter of Mr. Smith, and if they shall still continue strenuous in support of the Board of Controul, and think that the Court of Directors are not capable of conducting a mere pecuniary transaction, I will only beg leave to say, the sooner they are disbanded the better; their salaries are but a burthen to the Company, and their offices of little credit to themselves.

To those who are open to conviction, may I be allowed to throw out a few ideas on the subject of this mysterious secrecy.

What must become of the authority of the Company over their servants abroad under such a system? It cannot fairly be expected that much obedience will be paid to the Directors, when it is known, that their powers are limited to the mere routine of office, and that all the most material dispatches are transmitted without their knowledge. Once shew that they are become cyphers, and, destroying the idea of their consequence and dignity, you effectually overthrow the very foundation of respect and obedience. Thus low situated, their rank in the scale of India is at the mercy of committees. The same ship may carry
out

out proofs of the omnipotence of the Board of Controul, and the infignificance of the Court of Directors, and while the inftructions of the one are inculcating the leffons of peace, the orders of the other may found the declaration of war. In fact, intelligence of confequence will be known to the fervants before the mafters are acquainted with it, becaufe the difpatches of the Secret Committee may be made public in India when they are not even gueffed at here. So circumftanced, the authority of the Company will foon become ridiculous and an object of contempt. For protection and encouragement men will naturally look up to the fuperior, in preference to the controuled power, and what has been feelingly predicted by the Directors themfelves will quickly come to pafs—" the fervants will " learn to fpeculate on the probable judgment " which may be after formed on the propriety of " the original orders," and the *public* difpatch will be but little regarded till its concurrence with the *fecret* inftructions is made known.

It may be remembered that I ftated how feeble a fecurity was given for the Commiffioners not interfering with the commerce; I muft now argue more ftrongly, and add, that even the ambiguous protection afforded by the *words* of the act, is, by the *operation* of it, directly overthrown. Put the cafe that the Board of Controul fend a difpatch to the Secret Committee to be forwarded to India, which, through the medium of fome native Prince, materially affects the trade of the Company. By their oath the Secret Committee are reftrained from giving any information of the danger, and, as difpatches *received* in fecrecy are to be fecretly *anfwered*, it is obvious that the Court

Court of Directors can never know of the encroachment till they feel it in its mischief.—What now becomes of the boasted appeal? It is to all intents and purposes annihilated. No man can shew me a practicable method by which the Company can avail themselves of that clause in the act which says, "his Majesty in council "shall decide whether any proposed dispatch of "the Board is, or is not, connected with points on "which they have no authority." *The King cannot, without the voluntary information of the Commissioners, come at the bare statement of the fact, much less give a decision.*—The feelings of the India Company may, perhaps, without hazard be insulted, but decency should have forbid the name of Majesty from being sported with. How must it appear in the eyes of Europe, that an Act of Parliament which directs an appeal to the King, reduces him to the necessity of himself petitioning a subject to grant him the means of distributing Justice upon it!

While I am on this part of my subject let me take the opportunity to observe, that the *Prerogative of making peace and war* no longer exclusively flows in its usual channel; it may be exerted in India, by the secret powers of the Board of Controul, without any participation or knowledge of the Crown. A dash of the Right Honourable Commissioner's pen can set the whole country in a blaze, and none but himself and colleagues can quench the conflagration.—You Indian Princes who wish to enjoy the blessings of peace, profit by the hint! Come with offerings and pour your tribute into the lap of him who is the new Sovereign Disposer of fertility or desolation. In proportion as your allegiance to
him

him is proved, so may your Territories be protected or endangered, and, as your homage is neglected or paid, the Temple of the modern *Janus* may be open or shut.

Strange! that the loyalty of the people should be at the same time so vigilant and yet so blind! that they should see the danger of giving excessive power to one set of men who were to exert it *openly*, and yet transfer a prerogative to another who are to exercise it in *secret!* That a *public* assumption of the disposal of offices without the King's participation, should create almost an insurrection, and yet that the fate of an empire should, without jealousy, be subjected to a few individuals as a *private trust!* That they should defend their Sovereign against a distant storm of which he could gradually perceive, and prepare against the approaches, and yet assist to lay a mine of which the discovery and the mischiefs may be felt at the same unguarded moment! Let the Right Honourable Commissioner sit upon his secret throne for a few years longer, and who shall dare to counteract him? Dreaded by one half of the princes of India, and gratefully adored by the other; with the servants of the Company looking up to him with reverence, and the Directors regarding him with awe; having extensively scattered his connections abroad, and conferred obligations on hundreds at home; with the wealthy Plunderer his friend from fear, and honest Poverty clinging to him for advancement; in a word, with the whole Eastern empire in his grasp—what power is there in this country that can withstand his influence? *If the crown does not soon exercise its right to revoke the Commission, the season of kingly authority may be past.* I throw out this as comfort to those, who fear the present Bill will encrease the patronage of St. James's, and as a hint to such whose business it may be to watch over the rights of Prerogative.—Let me now, after asking pardon for this digression, return to the Secret Committee.

* The three gentlemen who constitute it are forced into the most cruel situation that can well be conceived. *As Directors* they take an oath, " ac-" cording to the best of their understandings, to give " their advice, counsel, and assistance for the sup-" port of the Company;" *as Secret Committee-men* they swear, " not to disclose or make known any " of the secret orders which shall be communi-" cated to them by the Board of Controul con-" cerning the levying of war or making of peace, " or *treating* or *negotiating* with any native Prince " of India." A multitude of cases might be put in which these two oaths would most materially clash, but I will beg leave to state *one*, the grounds of which are fresh in the Reader's memory. Suppose the dispatch relative to the payment of the Nabob's debts, as altered by the Board of Controul, had been sent to the Secret Committee to be forwarded to India (and the opinion of Counsel authorizes me to say that it might); what would have been their situation? Either they must have

' Let me not here be thought to mean any the most distant reflection on the present Members of the Secret Committee; indeed I need not do more than say that Mr. Manship is one, to prove that no disrespectful insinuation can be intended. I point of fact too, the mischiefs complained of did not shew themselves till after the three gentlemen, who now hold that trust, were sworn. I am convinced that the nature of the office was not, when it was undertaken, sufficiently considered, and my only object is to open the eyes of those who may be appointed in April next.

deviated

deviated from the *obligations* of *secrecy* to which they were *sworn*, or they must *silently* have *acquiesced* in a measure, " which," to use their own expression, " *their duty required* they should " *state* their *strongest dissent* to."—Indeed I look upon the Secret Committee, in the very nature of it, to be subversive of every principle on which business ought to be transacted. It is a constitution of three Gentlemen appointed to receive the pay of one description of men, for executing the commissions of another, and liable to be driven into that strange predicament, that they betray their trust when they discharge their duty. They may be forced to sign as their own opinion, that which their sentiments revolt at, and incur resentment and disgrace when they are entitled to compassion and favour. Though slaves they may be hated as tyrants, and, while they only discharge an insignificant agency, attract on themselves all the odium that attends on usurpation. With the most upright intentions towards the Company, they may be compelled to sign the death warrant of its rights, without being able to forewarn the victim of its danger, and in a word, become to the Board of Controul, what his *Mutes* are to the Turkish Bashaw, —the secret instruments of arbitrary power.— The characters of those who now are Commissioners for the affairs of India give us security against these mischiefs at present, but I maintain that under the operation of the Acts of Parliament such things *might* happen.

Let me now address myself to the Court of Directors as the Representatives of the East-India Company.

In

In return for all thefe infults, and encroachments, what advantage can you prove the Company to have received. What franchife has been confirmed to them, or what privilege explained in their favor? You will anfwer, your patronage is preferved;—let us fee how that ftands. You are not allowed to fend out one fervant to India, under the degree of Counfellors, until thofe already on the fpot are provided for, and I believe I am not far from the truth when I fay, that before that happens, your charter will expire. I admit you have the appointment of Counfellors at the different Prefidencies, but let me afk, without hinting at the weight which it is pretty well underftood the recommendation of the Board of Controul, privately fignified, would have, let me afk whether you would think it prudent to appoint any man, how extenfive foever his merits, who had the misfortune to be obnoxious to the Right Honourable Commiffioner? I fee you redden at the infinuation, and prepare to vindicate your independence. Well then, perfift in your own nomination.—Your favorite fhall take his feat with triumph—He is a Counfellor.—But let him now beware how he acts—Let *his* obedience atone for *your* obftinacy, and remember that *Protection* muft come from another quarter; let him bow and fubmit to the politicks of the reigning Powers, for if unfortunately he fhould be pronounced " *refractory,*" he *fhall be difmiffed the fervice and fent home to England!*

All that relates to Government or Revenue, is avowedly under the Board of Controul, from whence

whence it demonstratively follows, that to encrease the power of the Governor General, is to encrease the power of the Right Honourable Commissioners. By the late regulations of Parliament the number of the Council is reduced, and the Governor General enabled to act independently of them, hence the right of dismission becomes more valuable to the Board, and three out of four of your appointments are rendered insignificant. Let it be considered too, that the choice of Counsellors must be made from amongst those who have been twelve years resident in India, and the privilege of recalling will appear still more important.

As to the Governor General, I fancy it will hardly be contended but that your conduct in the nomination of him is regularly founded upon a sort of *Conge d'Elire*;—to this, however, you will answer, that you have the power of dismissing him at your pleasure. True, but to what end?—Of men qualified for so very arduous an office, there are but few to chuse from, and should you persist in the exercise of this right, you would soon be driven either to appoint him who is inadequate to his task, or support him who may insult you with impunity. May the Noble Earl who at this day presides over your affairs abroad, long superintend them! but do not forget that not even the virtues of Lord Cornwallis may be able to exempt him from the common lot to which his station, by the system now established, is liable. Whenever sufficient use shall have been made of his reputation as a soldier, and his fame for integrity as a man, it may afford but little security to him, that his conduct has been exemplary and his services eminent. Absolute dismission would indeed

indeed create an alarm, but the feelings of a veteran are nice, and a resignation might be easily provoked. Thwarted and privately teized on every measure, he might be driven to retire in disgust, and leave the Government of India to be managed by a successor better read in secret instructions.—If ever such an event should take place, the blessings of the Secret Committee, the power of the Board of Controul, and the value of your nominal right to appoint, will all, most probably, appear in their true colours.

As you are at length from practice, able to look upon encroachment without that violent indignation which formerly agitated you, may I be allowed to bring to your recollection the bill introduced by Mr. Fox in 1783, and presume to compare what you then so furiously resisted, with what you now so patiently submit to.

By *the bill of Mr. Fox*, the management of the India Company was vested in seven Commissioners, of whom Earl Fitzwilliam was President. Their office was to continue for four years, and their conduct was liable to the constant inspection of Parliament.—By *the bill of Mr. Pitt*, your affairs are governed by six Commissioners, of whom, in every paper but one which has been produced, Mr. Dundas appears to take the lead. Their powers gain additional strength every day, and no season is marked out to perfect their growth, neither, unless they chuse it, are their proceedings to be examined by any human creature except such as are sworn not to disclose them. What was there here to entitle the latter measure to the preference? Is the character of Mr. Dundas more respectable than that of Lord Fitzwilliam, or is a Secret Government, in the hands of the one, less liable to suspicion,

suspicion, than an open exercise of authority under the direction of the other?

Mr. *Fox* took the commerce, and lodged the superintendence of it in nine gentlemen, expresly nominated for that sole purpose.—*Mr. Pitt* neither takes it, or lets it alone, but, by a new species of ambiguous policy, leaves it to the King to decide on some future day to whose trust it ought to be committed. What is there of superior advantage to the Company in this? Or even if the *words* could be supposed to hold out any benefit, have I not shewn that the *operation* of the Act would effectually destroy it?

Lastly, by *the bill of Mr. Fox*, the servants were to be responsible to those who appointed them, but, by the construction of *Mr. Pitt's Act*, the right of appointment excludes the idea of authority.—I will not offend your understandings by an attempt to shew the absurdity of such a proposition.

I beg it may be understood, that I avoid all argument upon the effects which either of the bills may have on the constitution: Such a discussion would lead much beyond the limits which I have prescribed to myself, and therefore I will refrain from any opinion on the subject; but, as far as relates to *the Company*, I maintain the bill of Mr. Fox deserved the preference.—Its actions were open and avowed, those of the other secret and in the dark: Both dealt destruction to your chartered privileges, but the measure you resisted was as much superior to the interference under which you at present groan, as war is to assassination. In avoiding the Charge you fell into the Ambush, and I know of no other distinction than this, that instead of

[42]

dying honourably in the field, you are now reserved to perish in ignominious captivity.

I say to perish, because I hold it impossible you can survive the year 1790 when your charter expires, for every Proprietor must feel that your present constitution never will be renewed, nor is it to be wished it should. So strange a mixture of nominal authority and actual impotence is contrary to every principle on which a Government can hope to be prosperously conducted, and your total annihilation would be infinitely better than your present doubtful existence. Let the Board of Controul stand forward and openly take *all*, the *whole power* and the *whole responsibility*, and we know what we have to trust to; but a *secret*, *undefined* system, be it exercised by whom it may, will ever beget *suspicion*, and then follow jealousies, bickerings, and want of confidence, evils which are dangerous to the well being of every society, but which, to a commercial one, must ultimately bring destruction.

While it was supposed that the Proprietors would make a stand in defence of their privileges, and petition the justice of Parliament for redress, there were some hopes that your consequence might again be restored, and that you might return to your rank amongst the corporations of England. But the lot is now drawn, the only *piece* that could lead to connecting you from that — is compleated; and a negative power only, and the identification of the Company with the Board of Controul, has been virtually avowed.

Your situation therefore is now without remedy, and the picture of your past and present condition, when painted by the hand of truth, most mortifying. I will exhibit it faithfully, and then take my leave of the subject.

It is but three years ago that you attracted the notice of all Europe. You complained of an attack on your charter, and every man, from the King to the plowman, took the alarm. Such was your consequence at that period, that within a few days you carried all before you. You saw a whole Administration routed, a Minister supported in opposition to the House of Commons, a Parliament suddenly dissolved, and the name of the India Company sufficient in almost every borough in England, to over throw all considerations of property, connections, or Rank.

Mark the sequel! *You raised a power to crush yourselves*, and in the very moment of the most complete victory, you were obliged to submit to the conditions of the most disgraceful defeat; a defeat, compared to which, the overthrow you escaped from your original enemy would have been glorious. The attack of Mr. Fox certainly would have taken every privilege and franchise from you, but you would have lost them honourably, and the Company have expired with the reputation of martyrdom.— Better would it have been so to have died, than to be allowed to live on such terms as the present. The conquest obtained by the Board of Controul adds insult to injury, and having taken possession of your citadel and made you prisoners, compels you to walk in the Conqueror's train, dressed out in the pomp of your former dignity, like captives in a Roman triumph!

All the parade of your loſt conſequence remains while you are not able to call a ſingle privilege your own. Without knowing what your duty is, you are reſponſible to your conſtituents for the diſcharge of it, and though oſtenſible rulers of India, you cannot carry one meaſure into execution. With all the mockery of nominal power, you are deſtitute of vigour or efficacy, and you ſit with paper Crowns upon your heads, to copy diſpatches, and lament your fate!

POSTSCRIPT.

A REPORT having been industriously circulated, that the Board of Controul had made such concessions of power as to have satisfied the Company, I have thought it proper to add a few words on that subject.

At the General Court held the 7th instant, a motion was brought forward, " That a Com-
" mittee be appointed to consider of the means
" proper to be adopted, for ascertaining and more
" effectually preserving the rights of the Court of
" Directors and Proprietors."

In order to prove that there was no necessity for a measure of the kind, a paper was read, coming from the Board of Controul, which, on a cursory perusal, struck Mr. Rouse to be such a renunciation of the Secret Powers as the Company might be satisfied with. The motion on this was about to be withdrawn, but some little conversation happening to arise, a *second* Paper by accident fell into Mr. Rouse's hands, which so clearly proved the duplicity of *that* which had been held up as a concession on the part of the Board of Controul, and the little security the Company had for the future prevention of the encroachments they complained of, that the learned Counsel *desired to retract his first opinion*, and let the motion take its course. The consequence was, that it was sent to a ballot, and there decidedly *negatived!*

That I may not appear to keep any thing back, I have inserted the *first* Paper alluded to, in the Appendix

pendix No. VI. and the Reader will there also see that it is not my fault he is not gratified with a sight of the *second*.

As the case at present stands I can give no further information on the subject than, that the Paper which seemed to be advantageous to the Rights of the Company, was officiously produced and pompously read, while that, which took away from them even the appearance of security, was directed to the *Secret Committee*, and only came to light by the *mistake of a Clerk*. Let the world make its own comments.

APPENDIX I.

No. 1.

Demands of British Subjects on the Nabob.
24 *Geo. III. cap.* 25.

XXXVII. AND whereas very large sums of money are claimed to be due to British subjects by the Nabob of Arcot, in the recovery whereof, it is expedient that such assistance should be given them as is expedient with the rights of the said United Company, the security of the creditors, and the honour and dignity of the said Nabob; Be it enacted, That the Court of Directors of the said Company shall, as soon as may be, take into consideration the origin and justice of the said demands, as far as the materials they are in possession of will enable them to do, and that they shall give such orders to their presidencies and servants abroad, for completing the *investigation* thereof, as the nature of the case shall require, and establishing in concert with the said Nabob, such fund for the discharge of these debts which *shall be justly due* according to their respective claims and priority, as shall be consistent with the rights of the said United Company, the security of the creditors, and the honour and dignity of the said Nabob.

No. 2.

Dispatch, as originally drawn by the Directors, relative to the Mode of Liquidation of Public Debts, and Debts to European Creditors.

65. Pursuant to the directions in the late act of parliament, we have taken into our consideration the origin and justice of the demands of British subjects upon the Nabob of Arcot, so far as the materials in our possession have enabled us to do.

66. These demands are distinguished under the following heads, viz.
    The old debt,
    The new debt, and
    The debt to Messrs. Taylor, Majendie, and Call.

67. The Nabob himself, in his letter to Governor Palk, of the 12th December, 1776, has given the best account of the origin of the old debt that is to be met with upon our records, a copy whereof is inclosed, in which his right, after enumerating the causes which, from time to time, obliged him to procure pecuniary aids, declares, "that the sums lent him were truly and justly "lent him." The account of this debt in January, 1767, appears to be about 22 lacks of pagodas, at which time the interest thereon was reduced to 10 *per cent.* in consequence of our orders of the 17th of May, 1766. Not more than a fourth part of this debt, we understand, remains to be discharged, the Company having frequently recommended the case of these old creditors to the Nabob's favourable attention.

APPENDIX No. I.

68. It was not until the year 1776, that the Court of Directors were informed, that the Nabob had contracted a new debt, exclusive of the cavalry loan, to a much greater amount than the former. It is stated in 1777, at which time it was consolidated at thirty-five lacks of pagodas, bearing an interest of 12 *per cent.*

66. *Although we have repeatedly written to the Nabob, and to our servants, respecting the debt, yet we have never been able to trace the origin thereof, or to obtain any satisfactory information upon the subject.*

70. It is true, the Nabob has assured us in his letter of the 12th of August, 1783, " That the claims of his distressed creditors are the claims of justice, and whose demands he is bound by honour and every moral obligation, to discharge; that it is not, therefore, without great concern, he has heard insinuations tending to question the legality of their right to the payment of those just debts, which proceeded from advances made openly and honourably for the support of his own and the public affairs."

71. But notwithstanding the Nabob has thus admitted the fairness of these debts, yet, from the answer in his paper of requests, it may be inferred, that the Governor General and Council entertained a different opinion concerning them, when they thought it reasonable to require, that there should be an abatement of 25*l. per cent.* from such of the debts as may have been transferred, and that the whole should be discharged without interest. Besides, *suspicion respecting the nature of these latter debts, not very favourable to those concerned in them, have been dropped from high authority upon the spot.*

72. We

72. We do not mean to question the Nabob's right to issue his bond to whom he pleases, but *when those pecuniary transactions have relation to our own servants, who are bound to the Company for the performance of various conditions under certain penalties;* in all such cases, it is our indispensable duty to call upon the Nabob for every information upon the subject, and we make no doubt his Highness will see the propriety thereof, and afford us compleat satisfaction herein. We are in an especial manner impelled to procure such satisfaction, when we consider, that, for the discharge of these bonds, *the revenues of certain districts have been assigned to our servants, from a country, the defence of which rests entirely with the Company, who are therefore particularly interested in every thing that concerns its resources.*

73. For these reasons, we should have thought it our duty to enquire very minutely into those debts, even if the Act of Parliament had been silent upon the subject, before we concurred in any measures for their payment. But with *positive injunctions of the act before us, to examine into their nature and origin, we are indispensably bound to direct such an enquiry to be instituted*; and we therefore confidently hope and trust, that you will obtain from the Nabob and the creditors, the most satisfactory account thereof, before you lend the authority of the Company to any plan for their liquidation.

74. With respect to the 3d article we find that in April, 1777, the Nabob contracted a debt with Messrs. Taylor, Majendie and Call, of four lacks of pagodas, said to be advanced him, to pay the arrears due to his troops, for the repayment of which, the Madras Government engaged to be the security: *But the Court of Directors disavowed the transaction.*

APPENDIX No. I.   5

transaction. The accounts of the Nabob's officers will shew the several advances which were actually made in consequence of this loan, and whether the same were appropriated to the purposes intended.

75. It appears to us essentially necessary to call for these explanations, as the Nabob has asserted in his letter of the 22d of March, 1779, that the two years were nearly expired. Messrs. Taylor, &c. had not entirely discharged the arrears of those troops.

76. In the instructions given by the Nabob's creditors to Mr. Richard Joseph Sullivan, the 21st of February, 1781, on his proceeding to Bengal, we find the following statement:

	Pagodas.
The principal of the new consolidated debt is — —	35,00,00
The arrears of interest at that time	10,32,500
	45,32,500

The annual interest of this sum is stated at pagodas 5,43,900.

77. The letter from Madras of the 13th March, 1779, says, that besides the consolidated debt of 35 lacks, it is probable the Nabob may owe to individuals about 10 or 12 lacks more, including the money due to Messrs. Taylor, Majendie and Call, which additional sum takes in the whole of the Nabob's debt.

78. The following then is the most accurate statement of the Nabob's debts to his European creditors, taking the compound interest into the calculation, that we are able from the materials before us to procure.

Pagodas

APPENDIX No. I.

Pagodas 45,32,500 as above.
16,31,700 interest thereon to February 1784.
12,00,000 as above.

Pagodas 73,64,200

79. We are aware that the amount put down here, does not exactly agree with the Nabob's own statement of what he owes to his European creditors, as mentioned in his paper of requests to the Bengal Government, which produced the Treaty of April 1781. "Besides," says he, "the expences of the Company, the pay of my troops, the native bankers, my creditors, the Hindoo and Mussulmen securities, I am indebted about seventy lacks of pagodas to European creditors, both old and new, and people being under the protection of the Company."

80. In this state of uncertainty, as to the origin of the demand of the old and new creditors, particularly the latter, *(which precludes us from judging of the justice thereof)* and their actual amount, *the knowledge of which, we conceive, can only be obtained upon the spot*, we hereby direct our President and Council of Fort St. George, immediately upon the receipt hereof, to enter into a full examination as to the points mentioned in the act, viz. The *origin* and *justice* of these demands; also the exact amount thereof, *whether the sums were really and* bona fide *advanced*, and upon what particular occasion, also the *names of every individual creditor* who shall prove his debt *to the satisfaction of the said President and Council*.

81. Having

APPENDIX No. I.

81. Having compleated this enquiry, in which, as before-mentioned, the Nabob must be requested in our name to furnish every possible information, the whole of the proceedings must be transmitted to the Governor General and Council, who are hereby directed to take the same into their consideration to determine thereupon, and to establish in concert with the Nabob, through the medium of the President and Council of Fort Saint George, " Such a fund for the discharge of those " debts which shall appear to be justly due, ac- " cording to their respective claims of priority, " as shall be consistent with the rights of the " Company; the security of the creditors, and " the honour and dignity of the Nabob."

82. We think it necessary to acquaint you, that as many of the creditors, now residing in England, as shall prove to our satisfaction the origin and nature of their several claims on the Nabob, agreeably to the intention of the Legislature, their debts shall be considered as just and legal; and, so soon as the same shall have been substantiated, a particular account thereof shall be transmitted to you, in order that they may be included in the future plan to be formed for the liquidation of the whole.

From the great embarrassment, both to the Nabob's and to the Company's affairs, which the enormous amount of those private claims have occasioned, we are happy to find the Nabob willing to engage, not to incur any new debt with individuals; and we think little difficulty will be found in prevailing his Highness to enter into a positive engagement for that purpose. And though the Legislature has thus humanely interfered in behalf of individuals, as might otherwise

otherwise have been drove to great distress; yet we hereby positively prohibit any of our servants, or other British subjects under the protection of the Company, from making any farther loans of money to the Nabob, or any of his family, upon any account or pretence whatsoever, declaring, that we will not hereafter interpose our authority to procure satisfaction for engagements so entered into, contrary to these express directions, and the interest of the Company.

84. Since writing the above, the original register of the Mayor's Court at Madras, dated the 16th October, 1780, has been laid before us, specifying to whom, and at what time, the payments were made on account of the cavalry loan, amounting to pagodas, 4, 23, 436, 13, 26, also copy of a letter from Messrs. Call and Taylor, dated 25th March, 1779, to the Resident and Council, we send you a copy of these papers for your information, and to guide your judgment in the decision which you are to give respecting the justice of the claims of Messrs. Call, Majendie, and Taylor.

No. 3.

Ditto Dispatch as altered by the Board of Commissioners.

We next proceed to give you our sentiments respecting the private debts of the Nabob; and we cannot but acknowledge, that the origin and justice both of the loan of 1767, and the loan of 1777, commonly called the cavalry loan, appears to us clear and indisputable, agreeable to the true sense and spirit of the late Act of Parliament.

In

APPENDIX No. I.

In speaking of the loan of 1767, we are to be understood as speaking of the debt as constituted by the original bonds of that year, bearing interest at   per cent. and therefore, if any of the Nabob's creditors, under a pretence, that their debts made part of the consolidated debt of 1767, although secured by bonds of a subsequent date, carrying an interest exceeding ten *per cent.* shall claim the benefit of the following orders, we direct, that you pay no regard to such claims without our further especial instruction for that purpose.

With respect to the consolidated debt of 1777, it certainly stands upon a less favourable footing. So early as the 27th March, 1769, it was ordered by the President and Council of Fort St. George, that for the preventing of all persons living under the Company's protection, from having any dealings with any of the country powers or their ministers, without the knowledge or consent of the board, an advertisement should be published, by fixing it up at the Sea Gate, and sending round a copy to the Company's servants and inhabitants, and to the different subordinates, and our garrisons, and giving it out in general orders, stating therein, *that the President and Council did consider the irreversable order of the Court of Directors, of the year* 1714, *(whereby their people were expressly prohibited from having any dealing with the country governments in money matters) to be in full force and vigour;* and thereby expressly forbidding all servants of the Company, and other Europeans under their jurisdiction, *to make loans,* or have *any money transactions with any of the princes or states in India, without especial licence and permission of the President and Council for the*

time being, except only in the particular cases there mentioned; and declaring, that any wilful deviation therefrom should be deemed *a breach of orders, and treated as such*. And on the 4th of March, 1778, it was resolved by our President and Council of Fort St George, *that the consolidated debt of 1777, was not in any respect whatever conducted under the auspices or protection of that government*; and, on the circumstances of the consolidation of the said debt being made known to us, we did on the 23d December, 1778, write to you in the following terms: " Your account
" of the Nabob's private debts are very alarm-
" ing; but from whatever cause or causes those
" debts have been contracted, or encreased, we
" hereby repeat our orders, that the sanction of
" the Company, be on no account given to any
" kind of security for the payment, or liquida-
" tion of any part thereof, except by the express
" authority of the Court of Directors, on any
" account or any pretence whatever."

The loan of 1777, therefore, has no *sanction or authority from us*; and, in considering the situation and circumstances of this loan, we cannot omit to observe, that the creditors could not be ignorant how greatly the affairs of the Nabob were at that time deranged; and that his debt to the Company was then very considerable, the payment of which, they must alone most effectual way to postpone, by the appropriation or assignment of his specific revenues for the discharge of their own debts, in absence of that which the Nabob to discharge that of the Company.

APPENDIX No. I.

diency of keeping the subject of the Nabob's debts longer a-float than is absolutely necessary; when we consider how much the final conclusion of this business will tend to promote tranquility, credit, and the circulation of property in the Carnatic; and, when we consider that the debtor concurs with the creditor in establishing the justice of these debts, consolidated in 1777, into gross sums, for which bonds were given, liable to be transferred to persons different from the original creditors, and having no share or knowledge of the transactions in which the debts originated; and of course, how little ground there is to expect any substantial good to result from an unlimited investigation into them, we have resolved so far to recognize the justice of those debts, as to extend to them *that protection which, upon more forcible grounds, we have seen cause to allow to the other two classes of debts.* But although we so far adopt the general presumption in their favour, as to admit them to a participation in the manner hereafter directed, we do not mean to debar you from receiving any complaint against those debts of 1777, at the instance either of the Nabob himself, or of other creditors injured by their being so admitted, or by other persons having a proper interest, or stating reasonable grounds of objection; and if any complaints are offered, we order that the grounds of all such be attentively examined by you, and be transmitted to us, together with the evidence alledged in support of them, for our final decision; and as we have before directed, that the sum of 12 lacks of pagodas to be received annually from the Nabob, should be paid into our treasury, it is our order, that the same be distributed to the following arrangement:

That

That the debt be made up in the following manner, viz.

The debt confolidated 1767, to be made up to the end of the year 1784, with the current intereft at 10 *per cent.*

The cavalry loan to be made up to the fame period, with the current intereft at 12 *per cent.*

The debt confolidated 1777, to be made up to the fame period, with the current intereft at 12 *per cent.* to Nov. 1781; and from thence with the current intereft at fix *per cent.*

The 12 lacks annually to be received, are then to be applied;

1*ft.* To the growing intereft on the cavalry loan at 12 *per cent.*

2*dly.* To the growing intereft on the debt 1777, at fix *per cent.*

The remainder to be equally divided; one half to be applied to the extinction of the Company's debt; the other half to be applied to the payment of the growing intereft at 10 *per cent.* and towards the difcharge of the principal of the debt of 1767.

This arrangement to continue until the principal of the debt of 1767, is difcharged.

The application of the 12 lacks, is then to be,

1*ft.* To the intereft of 1777 as above, the remainder to be equally divided; one half towards the difcharge of the current intereft, and principal of the cavalry loan; and the other half towards the difcharge of the Company's debt.

When the cavalry loan fhall be thus difcharged, there fhall then be paid towards the difcharge of the Company's debt, feven lacks.

To the growing intereft and capital of the 1777 loan, five lacks.

When

APPENDIX No. I.   13

When the Company's debt shall be discharged, then the whole is to be applied in discharge of the debt of 1777.

If the Nabob shall be prevailed upon to apply the arrears, and growing payments of the Tanjore Peishcush, in farther discharge of his debts over and above the 12 lacks of pagodas, we direct, that the whole of that payment when made, shall be applied towards the deduction of the Company's debt.

We have laid down the general rules of diftributions, as appearing to us *founded in juftice*, and the relative circumftances of the different debts; and therefore, we give our *authority* and *protection* to them, only on the fuppofition, that thofe who afk our protection, acquiefce in the condition upon which it is given; and therefore, we exprefsly order, that if any creditor of the Nabob, a fervant of the Company, or being under our protection, shall refufe to exprefs his acquiefcence in thefe arrangments, he fhall not only be excluded from receiving any fhare of the fund under your diftribution, but fhall be prohibited from taking any feparate meafures to recover his debt from the Nabob. it being one great inducement to our adopting this arrangment, that the Nabob fhall be relieved from all further difquietude, by the importunities of his individual creditors, and be left at liberty to purfue thofe meafures for the profperity of his country, which embarraffments of his fituation have hitherto deprived him of the means of exerting. And, we farther direct, that if any creditor fhall be found refractory, or difpofed to difturb the arrangement we have fuggefted, he fhall be difmiffed the fervice, and fent home to England.

The directions we have given only apply to the three claffes of debts which have come under our obfervation. It has been furmifed, that the Nabob has of late contracted farther debts; if any of thefe are due to British fubjects, we forbid any countenance or protection whatever to be given to them, until the debt is fully invefligated, the nature of it reported home, and our efpecial inftructions upon it received.

(Signed)
   HENRY DUNDAS,
   MULGRAVE,
   WALSINGHAM,
   W. W. GRENVILLE.

No. 4.

Reprefentation of the Court of Directors.

6thly, Concerning the private Debts of the Nabob of Arcot, and the Application of the Fund of 12 Lacks of Pagodas per Annum.

Under this head you are pleafed in lieu of our paragraphs, to *fubftantiate at once the juftice of all thofe demands, which the act requires us to inveftigate.* Subject only to a right, referved to the Nabob, or any other party concerned, to queftion the juftice of any debt falling within the lift of the three claffes. We fubmit that at leaft the opportunity of queftioning, within a limited time, the juftice of any of the debts ought to have been fully preferved: And fuppofing the firft and fecond claffes to ftand free from imputation (as we incline to think they do) no injury can refult to

individuals

APPENDIX No. I.

individuals from such discussion: And we farther submit to your consideration, *how far the express direction of the act to examine the nature and origin of the debts has been, by the amended paragraphs, complied with,* and whether at least the rate of interest, according to which the debts arising from the Soucar assignment of the land revenues to the servants of the Company, acting in the capacity of Native Bankers, have been accumulated, ought not to be enquired into; as well as the reasonableness of the deduction of 25 per cent. which the Bengal Government directed to be made from a great part of the debt on certain conditions. But to your appropriations of the fund *our duty requires that we should state our strongest dissent: our right to be paid the arrears of those expences, by which (almost the country and all the property connected with it were preserved from falling a prey to a foreign conquerer) surely stands paramount to all claims for former debts upon the revenues of a country so preserved, even if the legislature had not expressly limited the assistance to be given to the private creditors, to be such as should be consistent with our own rights:* The Nabob had long before passing the act, by Treaty with our Bengal Government, agreed to pay us seven lacks of pagodas (part of the 12 lacks) in liquidation of those arrears *of which four lacks, the ——— ment you have been pleased to ——— ——— take away from us ——— ——— and give it to private creditors, of whose demands there are only about a sixth ——— which do not stand in a predicament that you declare would ——— ——— them to any ——— ——— a ——— ——— ——— ——— were it ——— ——— ——— as will more particu*———

estimate; until our debt shall be discharged, we can by no means consent to give up any part of the seven lacks to the private creditors, *and we humbly apprehend that, in this declaration, we do not exceed the limits of the authority and rights vested in us.*

CARNATIC REVENUES *and* DEBTS.

Lacks.

30. The Nabob's nett revenues stand estimated at —— —— £.1.200.000
As the utmost amount to be realized in times of peace, including all the districts under his Government, which lay to the Southward of Trichinopoly.

26. In 1776, the nett revenues came to 1.040.000

22. In 1777, the nett revenues came to no more than —— —— 880.000

After the ravages and depopulation which the Carnatic has undergone from the number of the husbandmen destroyed or carried off, there is little room to expect that its nett revenues can amount to the sum realized in 1777; but let it be supposed that the revenues to be realized on the return of peace shall be nearly to that of 1777, —— —— 800,000

There will then be to deduct from that sum the cost of the ten battalions, and of the usual garrison stores, amounting, together, to about £.200.000; also the twelve lacks of pagodas *per annum*, towards the discharge of the Nabob's debts, public and private, or 480,000—680.000, consequently the sum of £.120.000 will be all that can remain for the Nabob's Civil Government, and his own private use, a sum by no means sufficient for such purposes.

APPENDIX No. I.

On the other hand, if the revenues shall be short of the above-mentioned amount, and which will probably be the case, the proposed sum of twelve lacks cannot be realized to near that amount the year for the discharge of the public and private debts, and leave sufficient for the current demands.

The new debts consolidated, 25th Nov. 1777 (exclusive of the remaining part of the old debt of 1767, and the Cavalry Loan) amounted, according to the instructions from the creditors to Mr. Sullivan, in Feb. 1781, to   45.32.500

Nov. 1780, to Nov. 1781, 12 *per cent.* one year,   5.43.900

       50.76.400

Nov. 1781, to Dec. 1782, six *per cent.* 13 months,   3.29.966

       54.06.366
       3.24.382

1783, six *per cent.* one year,
       57.30.748
       3.43.844

1784, ditto
Pagodas   60.74.592

The Nabob, as appears by a letter from the Select Committee at Fort St. George to the Court of Directors, 13 March 1779, owed about 12 lacks more than the amount of these debts, and in which of course is included the remainder of 1767, and the Cavalry Loan. Nov. 1781, the Cavalry Loan is stated by the Nabob to be   Pagodas   5.03.370
       60.404

12 *per cent.* to Nov. 1782,
       5.63.774
       67.653

12 *per cent.* to Nov. 1783,
       6.31.427
       75.771

12 *per cent.* to Nov. 1784,
       7.07.198

The debt of 1767 was originally twenty-two lacks, the principal of this debt is stated to be paid off within a quarter part, or about five lacks, which remained due at the end of 1777. The interest unpaid in this debt cannot be traced, but it clearly appears to be largely in arrears, therefore supposing the principal and interest down to the end of 1784, not to exceed 12 lacks, the whole of the debts to that period, including the three several descriptions, will be ——— 79.81.790

New, ——— 60.74.592
Cavalry, ——— 7.07.198
Old, ——— 12.00.000
        Pagodas ——— 79.81.790

Since the amount of the debts admitted by the Board of Controul cannot be less than 79 lacks, probably more, when they shall all be made up to the 31st of December, 1784.

Now, admitting the old debts of 1767, with compound interest, after the rate of 10 per cent. to the end of December, 1784, to be only ——— Pagodas 12.00.000

The annual interest of 10 per cent. will amount to 1,20,000

Interest to be paid annually on the Cavalry Loan, at 12 per cent. principal Pagodas, 7.07.198, comes to ——— 84.000

The remainder, being the new consolidated debts, and amounting to Pagodas 60 lacks, the interest at six per cent. ——— 3.60.000

Interest to be paid annually in the first instance, ——— 4.44.000

The annual amount to be required of the Nabob for discharging the debts due to his private creditors, and to the Company, is stated at 12 lacks of Pagodas, or ——— £.480,000

The annual interest of the new consolidated Loan, and that of the Cavalry, which is to be paid prior to any demand of the Company, as now settled by the Board of Controul, on interest of these private debts amounts to about 180,000

The debts provided for, the remainder amounting to ——— £.300,000

is to be disposed of as follows:

APPENDIX No. I.

The one-half, or £.150,000, is to be appropriated to the reduction of the Company's debt, due from the Nabob, and the other half to the payment of the interest and principal of the old confolidated debt of 1767. The debt extinguifhed, the fame procefs is to take place for the exertion of the cavalry debt, thefe two debts making together £.760,000. with their growing intereft to the amount of £.80,000 a year, will take to the end of 1789, or 1790, to difcharge them, admitting the Nabob fhall make his payment of the firft 12 lacks by the end of 1783, (which can never be expected) and continue the fame annual advance, without reduction, down to the end of 1789, or 1790; becaufe any reduction of the 12 lacks muft tend to protract the difcharge of thefe two debts beyond the above period. But admitting that 12 lacks be regularly paid, in cafe the old debt of 1769, with its accumulated intereft, fhall exceed the amount herein ftated, and which is not at prefent afcertained, the extinction of thefe two debts would be equally prolonged beyond the end of 1789, or 1790, therefore *the Company, upon this plan, can have no profpect of being reimburfed in the enfuing fix or feven years more than £.900,000, or 1,000,000, of the money due from the Nabob, for the arrears of his current payments, and the expences incurred for the defence of the Carnatic, which, according to the ftatements already at home, and the charges to be brought to his account on the winding up the war, can be nothing fhort of three millions fterling, without any intereft charged upon it; whilft the debt due to the private creditors,* made up to the end of 1784, with compound intereft, and amounting to the fum of £ 3,500,000

£.3,500,000, will, *in six or seven years, have received an interest and principal upwards of 2,000,000, or of two-thirds of their amount, with compound interest, down to the end of* 1784. In short, under this regulation, *the Company will be to receive £.150,000, and the private creditors £.330,000 a year. And thus the public debt, carrying no interest, will be protracted to afford a preference to private debts, consisting of different descriptions, on the validity of a part of which claims the Board have declared,* they were contracted *contrary to the public orders of the Company,* and therefore could have *no sanction or authority* from the Court of Directors.

It is also to be observed, that if the Nabob shall, for three or four years to come, find himself unable to afford, from the current expences of Government, more than four or five out of 12 lacks towards the annual reduction of his debts and arrears, the Company and the creditors for the remainder of the old consolidated debt of 1767, the best established of the private debts, would receive nothing, as the growing interest on the new consolidated debt and the cavalry loan will take $4\frac{1}{2}$ lacks for its annual discharge; and nothing can more plainly shew the deficiencies in collections, than by observing, that the revenues, even under the management of Lord Macartney, have not been able to diminish the current arrears; but, on the contrary, they were, by the last advices, encreased as follows:

Arrears due in civil and military departments on the 31st of October, 1783, ——— £. 929,000
On the 21th of January, 1784, 1,273,000
exclusive of what may be due to the Southern troops

APPENDIX No. I.

troops (the accounts of which had not been received) and the expences of the Bengal detachment serving on that coast.

No. 5.

Rejoinder of the Board of Commissioners.

Sixth Article.——Arrangement of the Nabob's Debts to Individuals, and to the Company.

We think it proper, considering the particular nature of the subject, to state to you the following remarks on that part of your representation which relates to the plan for the discharge of the Nabob's debts.

1st. You compute the revenues which the Carnatic may be expected to produce only at 20 lacks of Pagodas, if we concurred with you in this opinion, we should certainly feel our hopes of advantage to all parties from this arrangement considerably diminished; but we trust that we are not too sanguine on this head, where we place our greatest reliance on the estimate transmitted to you by your President of Fort St. George, having then the best means of information upon the fact, and stating it with a particular view to the subject matter of these paragraphs, some allowance, we are sensible, must be made for the difference of collection in the Nabob's hands, but, we trust, not such as to reduce the receipt nearly to what you suppose.

2dly. For making up the amount of the private debts, you take in compound interest at the different

different rates specified in our paragraph; this it was not our intention to allow: And lest any misconception should arise on the spot, we have added an express direction, that the debts be made up with simple interest only, from the time of their respective consolidation clause.

3dly. We have also the *strongest* grounds to believe, that the debts will be, in other respects, considerably less than they are now reputed by you, and consequently the Company's annual proportion of the 12 lacks will be larger than it appears in your estimate. But even in your own statement of it, if we add to the £.150,000, or 375,000 Pagodas (which you take as the annual proportion to be received by the Company for five years to the end of 1789) the annual amount of the Tanjour peshcush for the same period, and the arrears on the peshcush (proposed by Lord Macartney to be received in three years) the whole will make a sum not falling very short of 35,00,000 Pagodas, the amount of 7,00,000 Pagodas for the same period. And if we carry our calculations further, it will appear that both by the plan proposed by the Nabob, and adopted in your paragraphs, and by that which we transmitted to you, the debt from the Nabob, if taken at 9,70,000, will be discharged nearly at the same period, viz. in the course of the 11th year. We cannot therefore be of opinion, that there *is the smallest ground for expecting to arrest event* as injurious to the interest of the Company, and if the measures were to be considered upon the mere ground of expediency, and with a view only to the wisdom of re-establishing credit and circulation in a commercial settlement, without any consideration of those motives of attention

APPENDIX No. I.

tention to the feelings and honour of the Nabob, of humanity to individuals, and of justice to persons in your service, and living under your protection, which have actuated the Legislature, and which afford not only justifiable, but commendable grounds for your conduct.

Impressed with this conviction *we have not made any alteration in the general outlines of the arrangement* which we had before transmitted to you: But as the amount of the Nabob's revenue is matter of uncertain conjecture, and as it does not appear just to us that any deficiency should fall wholly on one class of these debts, we have added a direction to your Governor of Fort St. George, that if, notwithstanding the provisions contained in our former paragraphs, any deficiency should arise, the payments of what shall be secured shall be made in the same proportion, which would have been obtained in the division of the whole 12 lacks, had they been paid.

As we have now transmitted to you our final directions on the whole of the matters in this dispatch, and as, on many of the instructions which are therein given to your servants in India, relate to points of the highest importance, and in which any unnecessary delay might be in the greatest degree prejudicial to your service, we desire *that you will for......... subject them to your different judgments.*

We have the honour to be, &c.
HENRY DUNDAS,
W. [ILLEGIBLE],
W. W. GRENVILLE,
MULGRAVE.

WHITEHALL,
3d Nov. 1784.

APPENDIX II.

No. 1.

Paragraph proposed by the Court of Directors, to be sent to their Presidency of Fort St. George.

Sent to the Board of Commissioners, 16th June, 1785.

IN reply to the two hundred and eighty-third paragraph of your select letter, dated the 5th September, 1782, relative to the request of your Chief Engineer, Lieutenant Colonel Ross, we cannot help expressing our very great surprize that, after we had twice put a negative upon his application for advanced rank, previous to his departure from England, he should have been induced soon after his arrival at Madras, to renew his aplication to you. In his letter to your Board of the 1st of July, 1782, he states, that we had permitted him " to return to his rank in the " service, which is next before Colonel James;" but Colonel Ross must have known that we permitted him, in the very words of our resolution, " To return to his rank of *Lieutenant-Colonel and* " *Chief Engineer at Madras*, but that he be not " allowed to rank in the infantry corps on that " establishment;" and that upon his subsequent request to rank as Colonel in the army by brevet, we resolved not to comply therewith. His urging you, therefore, to compliance with a request which he had previously decided on, was highly disrespectful to us, and we direct that you acquaint Lieutenant-Colonel Ross, of our disapprobation of his conduct on this occasion.

Extrac

APPENDIX No. II.

No. 2.

Extract of a Letter from the Right Honourable the Commissioners for the Affairs of India to the Court of Directors, dated June 27th, 1785.

WE have *expunged* the seventeenth paragraph of the draft No. 60, because *we cannot concur in your disapprobation of Lieutenant-Colonel Ross's conduct*, in renewing an application which we conceive to be founded on the constant usage of the King's military service. There are many testimonies on your records of Colonel Ross's long and faithful services, which entitle him to your favour; and we conceive his request goes no farther than to be put on a footing, in point of rank, with other officers of his standing at your Presidency, and not as a rank to be attached in future to the establishment of the Engineer Corps, or attended even in this instance with any new expence to the Company.

(Signed)   HENRY DUNDAS.
                 WALSINGHAM.
                 MULGRAVE.
                 W. W. GRENVILLE.

No. 3.

Extract of a Letter from the Court of Directors to the Right Honourable the Commissioners for the Affairs of India, dated the 30th June, 1785.

WE were equally surprized and concerned, that your Right Honourable Board should have expunged our paragraph concerning the conduct of Lieutenant-Colonel Ross, in having endeavoured

endeavoured to prevail upon our servants at Madrass, to comply with a request, which, previous to his departure from England, we, the Court of Directors, had twice refused upon his repeated applications. *This mode of appealing from the superior to the inferior authority, is so destructive of all government, that we should think we abdicated our trust, if such a conduct was permitted to pass without censure.* Sure we are that a moment's reflection will convince your Right Honourable Board, that *such a deliberate contempt of our authority, not only not disapproved, but indirectly applauded, by your Right Honourable Board refusing us permission even to reprehend, must lead our servants to imagine, that it is no longer their duty to obey those who possess the present authority in Great-Britain, but that they may safely speculate on the probable judgment which may be hereafter formed on the propriety of the original orders.* We shall not now discuss the propriety of our former resolutions, because we think the season for such a discussion is long since passed, but we beg leave to assure your Right Honourable Board, that we were not inattentive to the merits of Colonel Ross, when we formed the paragraph in question. We think we have acted with great moderation, yet this moderation must not induce us to forget the trust that is committed to our hands, consistently with which trust, it will be impossible for us to retain in our service any man, *whose contemptuous neglect of our authority we are not permitted to reprehend.*

APPENDIX No. II.

No. 4.

To the Right Honourable the Board of Commissioners for the Affairs of India,

My Lords and Gentlemen,

WE are extremely concerned to be engaged in any altercation with your Right Honourable Board, and much more that we should be impelled by a sense of duty to resist an authority which you have thought fit to exercise; but the present occasion appears to us *so momentous, and a submission on our part so destructive of all order and subordination in India,* that we must take the liberty to inform your Right Honourable Board, that no dispatch can be sent to India, which does not contain our final decision on the conduct of Lieutenant-Colonel Ross.

We have the honour to be, with great respect,
My Lords and Gentlemen,
Your most obedient, and
most humble servants,
Signed by order of the
Court of Directors,
THOMAS MORTON, Sec.

East-India House, the 2d July, 1785.

No. 5.

Extract of a Letter from the Right Honourable the Commissioners for the Affairs of India to the Court of Directors, dated the 7th July, 1785.

WE have given due attention to your letters, dated the 30th ultimo, and the 2d instant, and must, in the first instance, assure you, that we neither are, nor mean to be engaged in any altercation with the Court of Directors, and for that reason we avoid all observation upon the style of the letters you have been pleased to address to us. We shall endeavour faithfully, and conscientiously to discharge the duties of our situation, as chalked out to us by the authority of the Legislature, under which we act, without wishing to go beyond the limits which it has thought proper to prescribe *.

Upon the subject of Lieutenant-Colonel Ross, we agree with you, that his anxiety to obtain what he conceived to be justice, has lead him into an act of irregularity in stating his pretensions to the Governor and Council of Fort St. George, instead of respectfully conveying his request to you, his employers, through the channel of their dispatches. In this respect we think him culpable, and when we formerly gave you our sentiments upon this subject, it was merely to bring under your view the ideas we entertained of the justice of his claim, being perfectly aware that you are not bound to adopt these ideas, unless your own opinion should coincide with them. For reasons arising from the earnest representation you have made to us, you have our acquiescence to send out the paragraph as originally framed. We trust, however, that by this acquiescence, it will not be understood, THAT WE MEAN TO RECOGNIZE ANY POWER IN YOU TO TRANSMIT TO INDIA EITHER CENSURE OR APPROBATION OF THE CONDUCT OF ANY SERVANT, CIVIL

---

* As a specimen, see the conduct of the Board on the duties prescribed by the legislature, in the 37th section of the act relative to the claims of British subjects.

APPENDIX No. II.

OR MILITARY, EXCLUSIVE OF THE CONTROUL OF THIS BOARD. You very truly intimate to us, that it is in your power, without our permission, to dismiss Lieutenant-Colonel Ross from your service. The power you undoubtedly possess of appointing and dismissing your servants is a public trust, vested in you for the essential interests of the Company, and we are convinced, that the propriety of that trust will be fully justified by your *prudent* and conscientious discharge of a duty so delicate in itself, and so important both to the prosperity of the Company, and to the fortunes and characters of individuals thus placed under the protection of your justice.

(Signed)   HENRY DUNDAS.
                WALSINGHAM.
                MULGRAVE.
                W. W. GRENVILLE.

No. 6.

At a Court of Directors, held on Friday the 8th July, 1785.

ON A MOTION,

RESOLVED,—That the Right Honourable the Board of Commissioners for the Affairs of India, in their Letter dated the 7th instant, having given their acquiescence to sending the Court's paragraph respecting Lieutenant-Colonel Ross, under a declaration, " That they trust,
" that by such acquiescence, it will not be un-
" derstood, that the Board mean to recognize
" any power in the Court, to transmit to India,
" either censure or approbation of the conduct
                                          " of

" of any servant, civil or military, exclusive of
" the controul of the said Board," this Court
think it incumbent upon them to declare, that
they have not the most distant wish to resist the
controuling powers, delegated to the said Right
Honourable Board of Commissioners by the
Legislature; but, on the contrary, it is their
earnest desire to pay the most ready and chearful
obedience thereto, in as full a manner as such
powers were meant to be given by the Legislature: But at the same time, this Court further
think it right to declare, that as the appointment
of all officers, civil and military, is wholly in
the Company, together with a power of dismission, the right of reprehension for misbehaviour,
and more especially for every contempt of the
authority of this Court, from whom all appointments flow, must necessarily follow; and if this
Court should be controuled in the reasonable
exercise in the more mild power of reprehension,
they may be forced to adopt that of dismission,
for the very important purpose of guarding
themselves from insult, and preserving a due
subordination to the executive governing power
of the Company.

(31)

APPENDIX III.

No. 1.

Draft Paragraphs proposed by the Court of Directors, to be sent to their Presidency at Fort St. George.

WE have attentively considered your late dispatches, relative to the surrender of the assignment to the Nabob of Arcot, in obedience to your orders of the 9th December, 1784, and the manner in which those orders have been carried into execution, by the agreement of the 28th June last, and with your knowledge of the utter incompetency of the Soucar security, proposed in our before-mentioned dispatches to be taken for the 12 lacks, you acted very properly in stipulating, by the 4th article of that agreement, for the same kind of security as you were directed to demand for the Nabob's proportion of the current charges*. "We think, however, that the
" amount of this security, which is estimated
" only at six lacks of Pagodas per annum, is very
" inadequate, for the payment of the 10 lacks of
" Pagodas. We likewise consider, that the
" districts assigned by the 5th article were
" a part of those which had suffered most from
" the ravages of the enemy during the late war,
" and of course would be the least productive for
" some time to come. As, if you had failed in
" your endeavours to prevail on the Nabob to

---

* The paragraphs marked with inverted commas were expunged by the Board of Controul.

"name such districts as were in a more flourish-
"ing state, you acted very prudently in obtaining
"a stipulation, that if the deficiency exceeded
"what the assigned districts could make good,
"other districts should be specified in addition
"thereto."

We have likewise considered the arrangement of the kists in which the 16 lacks are to be paid into the Company's Treasury: You manifested a commendable attention to the Company's interests, by providing that the amount of the Nabob's share of the current charges should be exclusively paid with the first kist, and as much of the second kist as may be necessary to make up the four lacks of Pagodas. But, as we consider this agreement as merely preparatory to the final arrangement, which by our before-mentioned orders of the 9th December you were directed to negociate with the Nabob of Arcot, and the Rajah of Tanjore, we shall forbear to enter at large into a full discussion of this subject, until the receipt of the Definitive Treaty.

It is however proper to remind you, that by
"the first article of the Preliminaries, the Na-
"bob's current charges are settled for the pre-
"sent at four lacks of Pagodas *per annum*; we
"cannot help observing, that the Nabob has
"usually paid, upon the account of his current
"charges, previous to his making over the af-
"fignment of his countries to us, not less than
"five lacks of Pagodas *per annum*, and we are
"not aware of any reasons for departing from
"that rule in the present instance; but as you
"are shortly to have an engagement with his
"Highness, upon a new and permanent footing,
"and

"and as we do not wish to be too rigid, in
"exacting from the Nabob for so short a time,
"any sum beyond what has appeared reasonable
"to his Highness and to yourselves, we forbear
"to make any observations upon it, further than
"to say, that we are persuaded that you had
"good and sufficient reasons, which you will no
"doubt have communicated to us, for having
"altered the sum at which you have proposed
"to settle his Highness's current charges by
"the Preliminaries which you have already trans-
"mitted.

"There is also another part of the prelimi-
"naries to which we are persuaded you will ad-
"vert, when you come to settle the treaty itself,
"as it may be of consequence in a permanent
"agreement, tho' perhaps it may not in one
"which is merely temporary, viz. the power the
"Nabob has reserved to himself in the 5th ar-
"ticle, of keeping a full, exclusive, and ulti-
"mate authority over his Aumildars in all cases
"whatsoever. You will certainly recollect, that
"it was the constant opinion of your Govern-
"ment during Lord Macartney's administra-
"tion, that as long as the Nabob had that power
"vested in him, it was in vain for the Company
"to expect any benefit from the assignment of
"the country being made over in every other
"respect to them, altho' we flatter ourselves that
"his Highness and his successors will always be
"upon the best terms with the Company, and
"we consider their joint interests as inseparable
"from that of the Company in war, as well as
"in peace, yet to a nation looking to future (but
"we hope very distant) events, it is a conside-
"ration which we trust will by no means have
"escaped your attention."

APPENDIX No. III.

Extract of a Letter from the Board of Commissioners, dated 26th April, 1786.

No 2.

WE have expunged from your draft, No. 191, a confiderable part of what you have propofed to write to your Prefidency of Fort St. George, on the fubject of carrying into execution your orders of the 9th of December, 1784, with regard to the furrender of the affignment to the Nabob of the Carnatic, and their proceedings thereupon*. *As we think it more proper that fuch inftructions as it is now neceffary to tranfmit upon that fubject fhould go through the channel of your Secret Committee, we fhall fend a draft to them for that purpofe.*

(Signed.)   HENRY DUNDAS.
                      W^M. PITT.
                      W. W. GRENVILLE.

* The paffages fo expunged, are thofe marked with inverted commas in No. 1.

APPENDIX IV.

No. 1.

Case for the Opinion of Counsel.

" WE have expunged from your draft, No. 191, a considerable part of what you have proposed to write to your Presidency at Fort St. George, on the subject of carrying into execution your orders of the 9th of December, 1784, with regard to the surrender of the assignment to the Nabob of the Carnatic, and their proceedings thereupon. *As we think it more proper that such instructions as it is now necessary to transmit upon that subject, should go through the channel of your Secret Committee, we shall send a draft to them for that purpose.*"

Please to see the act of 24 Geo. 3. cap. 25. sect. 15. respecting sending secret orders concerning the levying of war or making peace, or treating, or negotiating with any of the native Princes, or States, in India.

Also sect. 37. of the same act by which the Court of Directors to take into consideration the origin, and justice of the demands of British subjects on the Nabob of Arcot, and to give orders for the security and discharge thereof, consistent with the rights of the Company, the security of the creditors, and the honour and dignity of the Nabob.

The Court of Directors conceive that the paragraph expunged by the Board of Commissioners, and proposed to be treated of by them in secret orders, are matters which *are expresly referred to the Court of Directors by the said 9th section*, and that even independent of such section, it was by no means agreeable to the *spirit* of the act, whatever may be the letter of it, that any negotiations should be *secret, except what related to peace or war*.

Your opinion is defired, whether the Board of Commiffioners for the affairs of India, are authorized either by the fpirit or the words of the faid Act of 24 Geo. 3. to correspond with and give directions to the Prefidency of Fort St. George, through the Secret Committee, directed to be appointed by that act, upon the fubjects treated of in the faid paragraphs.

No. 2.

Attorney General's Opinion.

There feems to me no doubt that the paragraphs expunged fall within the 15th fection, as relating to negotiations and treaties with a native Prince of India; and confequently, if the Board of Controul judge that the fame require fecrecy, they are authorized to direct them to be tranfmitted through the Secret Committee. The 37th fection has not in my opinion, abridged in the prefent cafe the power given to the Board of Controul by the 15th fection.

R. P. ARDEN.
June 13, 1786.

No.

No. 3.

Solicitor General's Opinion.

I do not see any just ground in the act of 24 Geo. 3. chap. 25. for making the subjects treated of in the paragraphs stated in the case, an exception to the general rule laid down in section 15, which extends to all treaties or negotiations with *any* of the native Princes or States in India, which may in the judgment of the Board of Commissioners require secrecy. The 37th section requires, that the Directors should as soon as may be, advert to the subject of British claims, and take measures for their adjustment and discharge, but if that is done by Treaty with the native Princes, and the Board of Commissioners deem any part of that Treaty a proper matter of secrecy, I conceive that the directions of the 15th section must be complied with.

AR. MACDONALD.

Lincoln's-Inn, June 13, 1786.

N. 4.

Opinion of the Company's Counsel.

By the 15th section the Board of Commissioners are constituted the judges of what matters require secrecy, relative to negotiations with any of the native Princes, and the Nabob of Arcot is unquestionably recognized in that character, as well by the public treaties of the country, as by the acts of the

the East India Company. I think therefore, as the act now stands, the Commissioners are authorized to transmit their orders through the Secret Committee, if such shall be their pleasure. It seems, however, not to have been a case within the contemplation of the Legislature at the passing the act; for the clause is manifestly directed to measures of hostility or negotiation with foreign Powers, which may require secrecy; whereas the Nabob of Arcot, (whatever he may be in form) is in effect the Administrator of the Civil Government of the countries conquered and defended by the British arms, holding these countries upon the implied condition understood and uniformly acted upon, of furnishing from the revenues the means of defence. *The arrangements taken with him, ought therefore to be made upon principles as fixed, and certain, and as open to discussion as the internal Government of the Province of Bengal.* The whole effect of the late Regulating Bill in constituting the two Boards of Directors and of Commissioners, the one proposing measures, and the other after representation finally deciding, will be lost, as far as concerns the Government of Madras, if the intercourse with the Nabob shall be confined to the Secret Department, because this intercourse involves directly the arrangements respecting the military force, and indirectly every interest of that presidency. The Directors cannot but recollect that the corruption of their Servants from that quarter, having already once overturned the Government of Madras, and being one cause of that war, which hazarded the loss of India, this intercourse will ever deserve their most vigilant attention. If the subject should appear equally

important

important to the Court of Directors as it does to me, I should rather advise an application to Parliament to explain this clause in the act, and confine it to its true object, negociations relative to war and peace, *than silently to relinquish all inspection into so important a part of the interests of the Company.*

GEO. ROUS.
May 2, 1785.

(40)

APPENDIX V.

No. 1.

At a Court of Directors, held on Tuesday the 13th June, 1786,

Samuel Smith, Esq. delivered in the following letter, viz.

Honourable Sirs,

I AM sorry to be under the necessity of entering any justification of my conduct on the records of the Company; but disapproving the acquiescence which has been given to the power now assumed by the Board of Commissioners, in taking upon themselves the final arrangement respecting the assignment of the Nabob's country, as a matter of *ficacy*, by a *forced construction,* and, as your Council has stated in his opinion, *on doubt of the clause by which the powers are defined respecting the Secret Committee,* as the subject neither involves the consideration of war, or peace, or negociation, or treaty, having a reference thereto, I must therefore protest against the exercise of that power, under such circumstances, in a manner as it tends to establish a secret system of government, dangerous in its principles, and subversive of the rights of the Company.

If arrangements are to be made with the Nabob's Princes or States, which do not involve the consideration of peace, or war, or any matter connected therewith, solely by the Board, as measures acquiring secrecy, because, by a forced construction of the clause, they may be termed negociations with native Princes or States, *the whole*

APPENDIX No. V.

whole political correspondence is taken from the Court, and given to the Board exclusively as a secret correspondence, which the Secret Committee of Directors are bound to transmit to India, but cannot *give any opinion thereon,* and which the Governors are directed to obey: Thus *almost the whole transactions of India may be concealed from the knowledge of the Court of Directors; nor can Parliament obtain any information upon the subject, if Ministers wish to with-hold it, without absolving persons from their oaths.*

The intention of the Legislature must have been, that the Commissioners should make only such things matters of secrecy, which, by being known, might be liable to be counteracted, such as orders for the levying of war, or the making of peace, or such negociations, and treaties which have a reference to either of the above, and which are universally admitted as necessary to the well being of the state, that they should for a time be with-held from public inspection; but it never can surely be contended, that *the liquidating a debt,* or the *settlement* of *a matter of account,* or *the receiving the security,* or *the assignments for the arrears of the revenue* can (because they might give rise to disagreements, which might eventually, though not probably, produce resistance) *fall within the construction of that clause.* If such is the meaning of that clause, *there is no transaction of any kind whatever, or concern in any department of the Government of India, which may not be asserted to have remotely some relation to native Princes or States,* and that may not be forced into the construction of that clause, and by that means *the whole political government of India be made a matter of secrecy.*

I am sensible the object of Mr. Pitt's Bill was to superintend and controul, with a view to prevent the abuses in India, and not to *wrest from the Company the political management of its affairs;* nor was it *then* urged, the proper Government for India was a Government of secrecy. The benefit likely to result from that measure was the mutual check that subsisted between the Board and the Directors. By the extension given to the power of the Board, by the *forced construction of that clause,* that check is entirely removed, and the *whole power lodged in the hands of the Commissioners, to be exercised at their discretion, without being liable to any inspection.*

It will be in vain to contend, that the patronage is secured to the Company by the Act of Parliament; if *the Government is secret,* it will be absurd to suppose, that the *patronage will be open,* or that those who have no voice in the measure will have much concern, if any, in the appointments; if they have not, to what evils, so often foreboded as dangerous to this Constitution, will not this mysterious Government of India expose us? And if this is to be contended as a necessary mode of managing and controuling the affairs of India, it will, in my opinion, give rise to a question, whether, under such circumstances of danger to the Constitution, our Indian possessions are worth retaining?

In thus objecting to the power claimed by the Board of Commissioners, I do not mean to dispute their power of controul, but contend, that except in the cases to which I allude, it ought to be *open and liable to inspection.*

I am also apprehensive that the trade, in order to make good the engagements now subsisting,

APPENDIX No. V.

must be forced to such an extent, as together with the export of bullion to China, (unless means can be found to supply that settlement from India) and the encreased import of manufactured goods, will involve many considerations respecting the essential interests of this country, as may render in its decision, the situation of a Director, and of a Member of the House of Commons, incompatible with each other. A public situation reduced *to the mere mechanism of official obedience* can afford but little credit, even by the most rigid discharge of its functions. Circumscribed as the power of the Court now is, and by the interpretation given to the clause to which I allude, *incapable of acting either with energy or effect, it must e'er long yield an easy surrender of its remaining rights, to the encroachments and vigilance of a more active controul.* Thus circumstanced, the office of a Director may be the subject of obloquy, and, though liable to a serious responsibility in the case of misconduct in others, is too subordinate to continue the post either of independence or honour.

It is, therefore, my intention to resign my trust to the Proprietors, conscious that whilst I held it, I endeavoured to discharge it to the best of my abilities, and with an integrity unimpeached.

I am, with great respect,
Honourable Sirs,
Your most obedient and
devoted Servant,
SAMUEL SMITH, Jun.

India-House, June 13th, 1786.

To the Honourable the Court of Directors, &c.

APPENDIX No. V.

No. 2.

At a Court of Directors, held Thursday, 15th June, 1786.

The Court now, according to order, proceeding to take into consideration a motion entered on yesterday's minutes, respecting the powers of the Right Honourable the Board of Commissioners for the affairs of India,

And the said motion having been amended, and standing as follows, viz.

" That it is the opinion of this Court, that the
" Board of Commissioners for the affairs of India,
" by drawing the pecuniary arrangements, with
" the Nabob of Arcot into the secret department,
" have extended the power given them by the
" 15th section of the act of the 24th of his pre-
" sent Majesty, (entitled, " An act for the better
" Regulation and Management of the Affairs of
" the East-India Company, and of the British
" Possessions in India, and for establishing a
" Court of Judicature for the more speedy and
" effectual Trial of Persons accused of Offences
" committed in the East-Indies,") beyond the
" original intention of the legislature, and, that it
" is expedient to apply to the legislature for a fur-
" ther explanation and more correct limitation of
" the said power."

It was moved, that the above motion be taken into consideration this day month.

And the question thereon being put by the ballot, the same passed in the affirmative.

No. 3.

APPENDIX No. V. 45

No. 3.

At a General Court, held on Friday, the 30th June, 1786.

RESOLVED, That the construction of the act of the 24th of his present Majesty, under which the Right Honourable Board of Commissioners for the affairs of India, have claimed to exercise the powers in instances before the Court, is *subversive of the authority of the Court of Directors, and the chartered rights of this Company*, recognized and confirmed by the said act, and *tends to establish a secret system of Government highly dangerous to interests of the the public and the Company.*

No. 4.

At a Court of Directors held Wednesday, the 29th of November, 1786.

THE Court now proceeding according to order of the 1st instant, to take into consideration the motion made on the 15th June last, respecting the powers of the Board of Controul,

The said Motion was read; also

The Resolution of the General Court, of the 30th June last.

It was then moved, and on the question, Resolved unanimously, That the Chairman, and Deputy Chairman, be desired to wait upon the Right Honourable the Chancellor of the Exchequer, to lay before him the resolution of the General Court of the 30th June last, and propose the following question, viz.

" IF

"If the Court of Directors with the authority of the General Court of Proprietors, shall think proper to apply to Parliament, to explain the powers of the Board of Controul with regard to Secret Correspondence, relative to the Country Powers of India, will you assist them in their application?"

No. 5.

Wednesday, the 6th of December, 1786.

THE Chairman acquainted the Court, that he had waited on the Chancellor of the Exchequer, and communicated to him the Resolution of the last Court, respecting an application to Parliament, as to the powers of the Right Honourable the Commissioners for the Affairs of India, and that Mr. Pitt signified his intention of giving an answer to the same in writing, in the course of the week.

No. 6.

Wednesday, the 13th of December, 1786.

THE Chairman and Deputy Chairman reported, that in obedience to the orders of the Court of the 29th ultimo, they had been this morning with the Chancellor of the Exchequer, who said " he cannot agree to the sentiments expressed in the resolution, concerning the conduct of the Right Honourable the Board of Commissioners for the Affairs of India, and does not see any ground for an application to Parliament on the subject."

APPENDIX VI.

No. 1.

To the Court of Directors of the United Company of Merchants of England, trading to the East-Indies.

Gentlemen,

OBSERVING of late that there has been confiderable *inaccuracy* in the correfpondence from India, which we in a great meafure attribute to fo much of your bufinefs, although no ways of a fecret nature, coming from the fecret department, we have inferted a paragraph in your draft, No. 294, for the purpofe of remedying that *inaccuracy*.

We have the honour to be,
Gentlemen,
Your moft obedient,
humble Servants,

Whitehall,
5th Feb. 1787.
(Signed) WILLIAM PITT.
HENRY DUNDAS.
MULGRAVE.

No. 2.

Copy of the Paragraph referred to in the above Letter.

In the conduct of your bufinefs we obferve, that a good deal of *inaccuracy* and *irregularity* arifes by fo much

much of your correspondence being addressed to us from your Secret Department. By this means an ambiguity is created as to the proper subjects to be directed to the whole Court of Directors, or the Secret Committee. To put an end to all *ambiguity for the future, we direct, that whatever is of a secret and confidential nature, and falls within the views and directions of the act of parliament, establishing a Secret Committee from among our number*, should be directed to our Secret Committee, but let all other subjects which do not fall within that description, cease to be addressed to us from your Secret Department, but let them come to us from your *Public Revenue*, *Commercial* or *Military* Departments, according to the nature of the subject with which it is connected, and by attending accurately to the arrangement of your correspondence under those heads, all ambiguity will henceforward be removed.

 Whitehall,   Approved by the Board.
5th *February*, 1787.
    (Signed)   Wm. PITT.
         HENRY DUNDAS.
         MULGRAVE.

APPENDIX VII.

No. 1.

Extract from the Proceedings at a General Court, held on Friday the 29th of May, 1767.

IT being observed, that it might be proper, that any Member of the General Court, might, for his more certain information, have copies of any part of the transactions of the General Court as he should desire, and the same having been debated, it was, on the question,

Resolved, "That it is the opinion of this Court, "that any proprietor of 500l. stock, may have a "copy of the minutes of any General Court, "paying for the expences of such copy."

No. 2.

To the Honourable Court of Directors.

Honourable Sirs,

I have to request a copy of the dispatch which was produced at the General Court, on Wednesday the 7th instant, and on which Mr. Reuse, the Company Council, founded his public opinion, that no substantial security was given by the Board of Controul for the future prevention of those measures, as in the secret department, which he found professed to disapprove of.

On an application to your Secretary's Office, I was informed, that the above paper could not be inspected by me, because it had not been *read* at the General Court; but, though a commendable caution in your officers, may on their part have justified this refusal of my request, I am persuaded the Honourable Directors will by no means with-hold any necessary information from a Proprietor, by adopting so very nice a distinction on so very interesting a point, but that, acting up to the spirit of the resolution of 1767, they will admit, that a paper, *produced at a General Court*, and there *argued upon by the Company's Counsel*, becomes to all intents and purposes *a paper which constitutes a part of the public proceedings of the Proprietary at large.*

I have the honour to be,
    Honourable Sirs,
        Your most obedient humble servant,
    (Signed)   GEORGE TIERNEY.
Grosvenor-Street, February 9th, 1787.

No. 3.

Mr. Morton presents his compliments to Mr. Tierney, and acquaints him, his request for a copy of the paper therein mentioned, was laid before the Court of Directors, who have directed him to inform Mr. Tierney, *they cannot comply with his request.*

East-India House, the 9th February, 1787.

www.ingramcontent.com/pod-product-compliance
Lightning Source LLC
Chambersburg PA
CBHW031122160426
43192CB00008B/1079